New
New York Interiors
Nouveaux
intérieurs new-yorkais

New
New York Interiors

Nouveaux intérieurs new-yorkais

Edited by | Sous la direction de | Herausgegeben von
Angelika Taschen

Texts by | Textes de | Texte von
Peter Webster

TASCHEN

HONG KONG KÖLN LONDON LOS ANGELES MADRID PARIS TOKYO

Endpapers | Papiers de garde | Vorsatz:
Jonathan Leitersdorf was able to transform an existing water-storage tank into a rooftop swimming
pool for his penthouse loft. | Pour son penthouse, Jonathan Leitersdorf a transformé la citerne sur le
toit de son immeuble en piscine. | Jonathan Leitersdorf machte aus einem ehemaligen Wassertank
auf dem Dach seines Penthouse-Lofts einen Swimmingpool.
Photo: Bärbel Miebach/baerbelmiebach.com
Page 2 | Page 2 | Seite 2:
Architect Lee Mindel designed a "double-helix" stainless steel and concrete staircase to the roof
of his Flatiron District penthouse. | L'architecte Lee Mindel a créé un escalier à « double hélice »
en acier et béton pour mener au toit de son penthouse dans le quartier du Flatiron | Der Architekt
Lee Mindel hat diese „Doppel-Helix"-Treppe aus Edelstahl und Beton entworfen. Sie führt auf
das Dach seines Penthouses im Flatiron District.
Photo: Michael Moran
Page 7 | Page 7 | Seite 7:
Swiss artist Sylvie Fleury's carbon-fibre "Mushrooms" sit on art dealer Michael Fuchs' Chelsea
terrace. | « Mushrooms », une sculpture en fibres de carbone de la Suissesse Sylvie Fleury, orne la
terrasse du marchand d'art Michael Fuchs à Chelsea. | „Mushrooms" aus Kohlenstofffaser der
Schweizer Künstlerin Sylvie Fleury auf der Terrasse des Kunsthändlers Michael Fuchs in Chelsea.
Photo: François Halard

© 2008 TASCHEN GmbH
Hohenzollernring 53, D-50672 Köln
www.taschen.com

Compilation, editing & layout: Angelika Taschen, Berlin
General Project Manager: Stephanie Bischoff, Cologne
Texts: Peter Webster, New York
French translation: Philippe Safavi, Paris
German translation: Simone Ott Caduff, California
Production: Thomas Grell, Cologne

Printed in China
ISBN 978-3-8365-0485-0
ISBN 978-3-8365-0487-4 (edition with French cover)

Contents
Sommaire
Inhalt

New York revisited

Preface by Angelika Taschen

New York revisité

Préface de Angelika Taschen

New York revisited

Vorwort von Angelika Taschen

The first volume of "New York Interiors" was published over ten years ago, in a completely different era of the USA, when Bill Clinton was Democratic President and 9/11 hadn't happened. In the meantime, the country has changed radically. New York is and always will be New York, but even here the energy has shifted. The terror attack of 2001 had a devastating effect on the city, yet just such a trauma often gives rise to change. Today the city is much less focused on money and the making of it – a great improvement, in my opinion. After the heyday of the nineties, even Wall Street has sunk into a depression. Now you can live here very exclusively, but not expensively, while at the same time taking advantage of the countless opportunities still around – a life style that will always attract creative intellects. The interiors I have chosen for this book reflect the abundance of artists in New York, the innumerable galleries and blue-chip art collectors, all making the city such a great place to live in. The rents in Manhattan are very high, and ultra-luxurious tower blocks are still being built. I have included one of these apartments in this book as an example for this style: Herbert Sambol's apartment, furnished and decorated by Lee Mindel and located in Perry Street Towers on West Side Highway, a project by the architect Richard Meier. This is one of the reasons Brooklyn, Williamsburg or Harlem are becoming more and more appealing, and urban neighborhoods are springing up in these districts. The examples I have taken here are Cary Leibowitz's eccentric town house in Harlem, the small loft of furniture designer Tyler Hays in Williamsburg, and Lorenzo Salazar's delightful apartment above a nail studio in Brooklyn. Famous artists just love living in Manhattan, artists such as Alex Katz in his elegantly low-key loft-atelier, Julian Schnabel in the Venetian dream of his own making in the West Village, or the young shooting star, Terence Koh, in his experimental house in Chinatown. But other creative intellects from all walks of life find their way to the Big Apple and love the life there, be it the designer legend Vladimir Kagan, the musician Rufus Wainwright, the actors Joel Grey and Julianne Moore, the gastronomy genius Sean MacPherson, or, last but not least, the porno-star Vanessa del Rio. They all feel the same: "I love NY!"

Le premier « New York Interiors » a vu le jour il y a plus de dix ans, à une autre époque, celle du président démocrate Bill Clinton, et avant les attentats du 11 septembre 2001. Depuis, le pays a beaucoup changé, New York est resté New York, bien sûr, mais son énergie n'est plus la même. Le 11 septembre a stigmatisé la ville, pourtant un choc offre souvent un terrain fécond aux changements. Aujourd'hui, et c'est un atout pour elle, les yeux sont beaucoup moins fixés sur l'argent, et Wall Street qui s'épanouissait encore durant les années 1990 est en baisse. On peut donc vivre ici de manière originale mais aussi bon marché ; en même temps les possibilités sont restées infinies, ce qui attire les créatifs. Les intérieurs sélectionnés pour cet ouvrage reflètent la profusion qui règne ici, la présence des milliers d'artistes, des galeries innombrables et des collectionneurs Blue-chip qui rendent cette ville si agréable à vivre. À Manhattan, les prix des logements sont très élevés et on construit des appartements super-luxueux tels ceux qu'abritent les « Perry Street Towers » de Richard Meier, sur la West Side Highway. Ils sont représentés de manière exemplaire dans le présent ouvrage par celui de Herbert Sambol décoré par Lee Mindel. C'est la raison pour laquelle de plus en plus de gens sont attirés par Brooklyn, Williamsburg ou Harlem, où des neighborhoods urbains ont entre-temps vu le jour. Il faut voir ici la townhouse excentrique de Cary Leibowitz à Harlem, le petit loft du designer de mobilier Tyler Hays à Williamsburg ou le charmant appartement de Lorenzo Salazar situé au-dessus d'une onglerie. De grands artistes sont fous de Manhattan, ainsi Alex Katz qui vit dans un atelier-loft à l'élégance minimaliste, Julian Schnabel dans le rêve vénitien qu'il a lui-même créé à West Village ou la jeune shooting-star Terence Koh dans sa maison expérimentale de China Town. Mais d'autres créateurs en tout genre aiment Big Apple, c'est le cas du designer mythique Vladimir Kagan, du musicien Rufus Wainwright, des acteurs Joel Grey et Julianne Moore, du génie de la gastronomie Sean MacPherson, et, last but not least, de la star du porno Vanesso del Rio. Tous peuvent dire en chœur : I love NY !

Der erste Band „New York Interiors" entstand vor über zehn Jahren in einer anderen Ära der Vereinigten Staaten als noch der demokratische Präsident Bill Clinton regierte und vor 9/11. Seitdem hat sich das Land stark verändert, New York ist zwar immer noch New York, aber auch hier hat sich die Energie verwandelt. Der Terroranschlag von 2001 hat die Stadt stigmatisiert. Doch eine Erschütterung ist oft fruchtbarer Boden für Veränderungen. Die Stadt ist heute, sehr zu ihrem Vorteil, weniger auf Geld fixiert, auch die Wall Street, die in den 1990ern noch blühte, befindet sich in einem Tief. So kann man hier sehr exklusiv, aber auch preiswert leben, gleichzeitig gibt es nach wie vor unendliche Möglichkeiten – das zieht Kreative magisch an. Die von mir für dieses Buch ausgewählten Interieurs reflektieren die Überfülle New Yorks an Tausenden Künstlern, unzähligen Galerien und Blue-chip-Kunstsammlern, die diese Stadt so lebenswert machen. In Manhattan sind die Preise für Wohnungen sehr hoch, und es werden ultraluxuriöse Apartmenthochhäuser gebaut, wie die „Perry Street Towers" am West Side Highway von Richard Meier, die in diesem Buch mit der von Lee Mindel eingerichteten Wohnung von Herbert Sambol exemplarisch vertreten sind. Deshalb zieht es immer mehr Leute nach Brooklyn, Williamsburg oder Harlem, wo inzwischen urbane Neighborhoods entstanden sind. Als Beispiele sind zu sehen das exzentrische Townhouse von Cary Leibowitz in Harlem, das kleine Loft des Möbeldesigners Tyler Hays in Williamsburg oder die charmante Wohnung über einem Nagelstudio in Brooklyn von Lorenzo Salazar. In Manhattan leben mit großer Begeisterung bedeutende Künstler, wie Alex Katz in seinem elegant-reduziertem Loft-Atelier, Julian Schnabel in dem von ihm selbst geschaffenen venezianischen Traum im West Village oder der junge Shootingstar Terence Koh in seinem experimentellen Haus in Chinatown. Aber auch andere kreative Geister aller Couleur lieben den Big Apple, wie die Designlegende Vladimir Kagan, der Musiker Rufus Wainwright, die Schauspieler Joel Grey und Julianne Moore, das Gastronomiegenie Sean MacPherson und last, not least der Pornostar Vanessa del Rio, für die alle das Gleiche gilt: I love NY!

Qui imaginerait que ce loft serein est la demeure de Marina Abramovic, artiste connue pour ses performances dérangeantes, parfois violentes ? Cet appartement de 280 mètres carrés abrite peu de meubles et aucune œuvre d'art, hormis quelques grands dessins en cours de son mari, Paolo Canevari, qui utilise l'espace comme un atelier. Sitôt les dessins achevés, ils doivent partir car, comme l'explique Abramovic : « Un artiste a besoin d'espaces vides afin d'y projeter les images qu'il n'a pas encore créé. » Elle vivrait volontiers dans des pièces vides. « J'aime l'idée d'une architecture toute en espace. Mon mari, lui, aime les objets, notamment ceux des années 1950 et 1960. » D'ailleurs, c'est lui qui a conçu la table de salle à manger qui, contrairement à ses dessins, a eu le droit de rester.

Marina Abramovic & Paolo Canevari

Who could guess that this serene loft is the home of Marina Abramovic, the performance artist famed for her disturbing, sometimes violent, pieces? The 3,000-square-foot apartment has little furniture and no art, except for a few large drawings, works-in-progress by Abramovic's husband, Paolo Canevari, who uses the loft as a studio. But once the drawings are finished, out they go. "As an artist, you need empty spaces so you can project images that haven't been made yet," says Abramovic, who could live without any furniture. "I love the idea of light and space as architecture," which is a good description of her airy loft. "My husband really likes objects, especially from the 1950s and 1960s." In fact, he designed the dining table, which, unlike his drawings, is allowed to stay.

Die Performancekünstlerin Marina Abramovic ist für ihre aufwühlenden, leidenschaftlichen Auftritte bekannt. Umso mehr erstaunt, wie himmlisch ruhig ihr Loft ist. Das 280 Quadratmeter große Apartment wirkt spartanisch: kaum Möbel, keine Kunst – außer die großen Zeichnungen, an denen Abramovics Mann, Paolo Canevari, jeweils aktuell arbeitet. Er mag es, in den frühen Morgenstunden zu zeichnen, und benutzt das Loft auch als Atelier. Sind die Zeichnungen einmal fertig, gehen sie aus dem Haus. „Ein Künstler braucht leere Flächen, um seinen inneren Bildern Gestalt zu geben", erklärt Abramovic, die am liebsten ganz ohne Möbel leben möchte. Ihrer Vorstellung von Architektur genügt – wie ihr luftiges, helles Loft zeigt – einzig Licht und Raum. „Mein Mann dagegen liebt Objekte, speziell aus den 1950ern und 1960ern." Und er hat den wunderbaren Esstisch entworfen, der anders als seine Zeichnungen im Loft bleiben darf.

Previous pages: The loft gets so much light that the window blinds are often lowered. Canevari designed the dining table; the vintage Italian chairs are in the style of Gio Ponti.
Above: The kitchen is tucked between the living area and the bedroom.
Right: Canevari works on "Burning Vespa," which, like "God Year" to the right, will be removed once it is finished.
Facing page: Sitting area furniture includes sofas by Patricia Urquiola, a vinyl armchair and a coffee table, both 1950s American.

Pages précédentes : Le loft est tellement inondé de lumière que les stores restent souvent baissés. Canevari a dessiné la table de salle à manger. Les chaises italiennes vintage sont dans le style de Gio Ponti.
En haut : La cuisine est nichée entre le séjour et la chambre.
À droite : Canevari travaille sur « Burning Vespa » qui, comme « God Year », sur la droite, sera décroché du mur une fois terminé.
Page de droite : Dans le coin salon, les meubles incluent un canapé de Patricia Urquiola, un fauteuil en vinyle et une table basse, toutes deux américaines des années 1950.

Vorhergehende Seiten: Die Fenster lassen so viel Licht in das Loft, dass die Rollos meist heruntergelassen sind. Der Esstisch ist ein Entwurf von Canevari. Die italienischen Stühle dazu sind im Gio-Ponti-Stil.
Oben: Eingenistet zwischen Essraum und Schlafzimmer liegt die Küche.
Rechts: Canevari zeichnet gerade an „Burning Vespa". Wie „God Year" (rechts) wird das Werk, sobald es fertig ist, aus dem Loft geschafft.
Gegenüberliegende Seite: Im Wohnbereich steht ein Sofasystem von Patricia Urquiola, ein amerikanischer mit Vinyl bezogener Sessel und ein Klubtisch aus den 1950ern.

Les galeries d'art contemporain sont toujours blanches et minima-listes. Celle de Marianne Boesky à Chelsea ne fait pas exception. En revanche, l'appartement de 335 mètres carrés à l'étage, où elle vit avec son mari Liam Culman et leur fille, n'a rien d'austère. Meubles anciens, tissus imprimés, moulures et, dans une pièce, un papier peint créent un décor conventionnel qui contraste avec les œuvres auda-cieuses accrochées au mur. Boesky est moderniste, alors que Culman est plus traditionnel. L'architecte Deborah Berke, qui a conçu le bâti-ment abritant la galerie et l'appartement, a donc opté pour un chic discret qui représente un compromis heureux entre leurs deux esthé-tiques. Jouant avec les couleurs, les textures et les proportions, elle a créé une demeure qui vénère l'art sans sacrifier celui de vivre.

Marianne Boesky & Liam Culman

Contemporary art galleries are always white, minimalist environ-ments, and Chelsea dealer Marianne Boesky's space is no different. Upstairs, however, the 3,600-square-foot apartment Boesky shares with her husband, Liam Culman, and daughter is much less austere. Traditional furniture, patterned fabrics, architectural moldings, and, in one room, wallpaper, create a more conventional setting than expected, given the edgy art on the walls. Boesky is a mod-ernist – but Culman has more traditional tastes. The chic interiors represent a happy compromise between the aesthetics, thanks to Deborah Berke, the architect of the building housing Boesky's gallery and apartment. Playing with color, texture and proportion, Berke has created a home that reveres art without overlooking life.

Galerien für zeitgenössische Kunst sind meist weiß und minimalis-tisch. Auch der Ausstellungsraum der Galeristin Marianne Boesky in Chelsea ist nicht anders. Mit ihrer Privatwohnung hält sie es aber weniger streng: Boesky lebt mit ihrem Mann Liam Culman und ihrer Tochter auf 335 Quadratmeter im Stockwerk über der Galerie in konventionellerem Rahmen als die außergewöhnliche Kunst an den Wänden vermuten ließe. Zwar liebt Boesky die Moderne, dennoch lebt sie zwischen traditionellen Möbeln, gemusterten Stoffen, Zier-leisten – und sogar Tapeten: „etwas Neues für mich!" Dies ihrem Gatten, Liam Culman, zuliebe, der es eher traditionell mag. Archi-tektin Deborah Berke, die das ganze Wohnhaus und auch Boeskys Galerie entwarf, verband die beiden Geschmäcker zu einem glück-lichen Kompromiss. Sie spielte mit Farben, Strukturen, Proportionen und schaffte ein unaufgeregt schickes, zeitloses Interieur für die Be-wohner und ihre Kunst.

Left: The white brick building architect Deborah Berke designed houses Boesky's gallery and apartment.
Below: Boesky's husband, Liam Culman, has a traditional gentleman's study, although it has sculptures by Robert Gober and Nara on the bookshelves.
Facing page: A Nara dog stands on the roof terrace, which was designed by Paula Hayes, an artist who specializes in making gardens as site-specific artworks.

À gauche : Le bâtiment en briques blanches de Deborah Berke abrite la galerie et l'appartement de Boesky.
En bas : Le mari de Boesky, Liam Culman, a un bureau traditionnel de gentleman, mais sa bibliothèque accueille néanmoins des sculptures de Robert Gober et de Nara.
Page de droite : La terrasse sur le toit a été conçue par Paula Hayes, artiste et paysagiste. Au premier plan, un chien de Nara.

Links: Das weiß gestrichene Backsteinhaus von Architektin Deborah Berke. Sie hat auch die Interieurs der Galerie und der Wohnung im gleichen Gebäude gestaltet.
Unten: Das Studierzimmer von Boeskys Ehemann, Liam Culman. Trotz Skulpturen von Robert Gober und Nara im Bücherregal regiert hier der Geschmack eines Gentlemans alter Schule.
Gegenüberliegende Seite: Hundeskulptur von Nara auf der von der Künstlerin Paula Hayes entworfenen Dachterrasse.

Previous pages: In the living room, what looks like striped wallpaper is in fact a work by French artist Daniel Buren; a painting by Yoshitomo Nara hangs above the Deborah Berke-designed honey onyx fireplace, in front of which sits Yves Klein's "Table rose."

Pages précédentes : Les murs du séjour ne sont pas recouverts d'un papier peint à rayures, mais d'une œuvre du français Daniel Buren. Au-dessus de la cheminée en onyx miel dessinée par Deborah Berke, une toile de Yoshitomo Nara. Devant, la « Table rose » d'Yves Klein.

Vorhergehende Seiten: Was im Wohnzimmer wie eine gestreifte Tapete aussieht, ist ein Werk des französischen Künstlers Daniel Buren. Über dem Kamin aus Onyx – ein Entwurf von Deborah Berke – hängt ein Bild von Yoshitomo Nara. Davor der „Table rose" von Yves Klein.

New New York Interiors   Marianne Boesky & Liam Culman

Left: An Eero Saarinen pedestal table and Harry Bertoia wire chairs sit in front of a high-backed custom-made sofa in the kitchen's breakfast area.
Below: Above a 1950s Italianate mirrored night stand, an adjustable wall sconce provides reading light in the master bedroom.

À gauche : Dans le coin du petit déjeuner de la cuisine, une table ronde d'Eero Saarinen et des chaises métalliques de Harry Bertoia devant un canapé à haut dossier réalisé sur mesure.
En bas : Dans la chambre des maîtres, au-dessus d'une table de chevet en miroir italianisante des années 1950, une applique orientable pour pouvoir lire dans son lit.

Links: In der Frühstücksecke der Küche stehen um ein Eero-Saarinen-Tisch Stühle von Harry Bertoia. Dahinter ein Sofa mit hoher Lehne, eine Spezialanfertigung.
Unten: Sorgt im großen Schlafzimmer für Leselicht: die Wandleuchte über dem verspiegelten Nachttisch im italienischen Stil aus den 1950ern.

Previous pages: Adam Helms's "4 Untitled Portraits" hang above the doorway between the living and dining rooms. Two types of antique chairs – tall walnut-stained ones, and round-backed faux-bamboo ones – are used at the custom-made dining table, on which sit glass terrariums by Paula Hayes; Damien Hirst's "Hope II" hangs on the wall.
Facing page: The tree-patterned wallpaper in the powder room is English.

Pages précédentes : Au-dessus de la porte qui relie le séjour à la salle à manger, « 4 Untitled Portraits » d'Adam Helms. Autour de la table de salle à manger réalisée sur mesure, de hautes chaises anciennes teintées en noyer et d'autres plus petites au dossier rond et en imitation de bambou. Sur la table, des mini-serres en verre de Paula Hayes. Au mur, « Hope II » de Damian Hirst.
Page de gauche : Dans le cabinet de toilette, le papier peint représentant une forêt hivernale est anglais.

Vorhergehende Seiten: Die „4 Untitled Portraits" von Adam Helms hängen über dem Durchgang zwischen Wohn- und Esszimmer. Zwei Stuhlarten stehen rund um den maßgefertigten Esstisch: die hohen walnussbraun gebeizten Stühle und die mit runder Lehne aus Bambus-Imitat. Auf dem Tisch stehen Glaserrarien von Paula Hayes. An der Wand „Hope II" von Damien Hirst.
Gegenüberliegende Seite: Die Baummuster-Tapete in der Toilette stammt aus England.

Muriel Brandolini a quitté le Viêtnam très jeune mais cette décoratrice vietnamo-franco-vénézuélienne n'a pas oublié ses racines sud-asiatiques ni les autres lieux où elle a grandi, dont la Martinique et la France, avant d'arriver aux États-Unis. Si on ajoute à cela un mari banquier italien, Nuno, on ne s'étonne plus que l'hôtel particulier de trois étages dans le Upper East Side qu'elle a restauré pour lui et leurs deux enfants offre le meilleur de la décoration internationale. Elle a marié dans cet hôtel de 1890 des meubles des 18e, 19e et 20e siècles venus des quatre coins de la planète dans des pièces tapissées ou peintes de couleurs vibrantes. « Je finis toujours par les murs », confie-t-elle. « Je n'aborde jamais un projet avec des idées préconçues. Je suis simplement mon instinct du moment. »

Muriel Brandolini

Muriel Brandolini hasn't lived in Vietnam since she was child, but the Vietnamese-French-Venezuelan interior designer hasn't forgotten her Southeast Asian roots — or any other part of a cosmopolitan upbringing that included stints in Martinique and France before coming to the United States as a young adult. Throw her Italian banker husband, Nuno, into the mix, and you see why the 1890 four-story Upper East Side townhouse she renovated for him and their two children is all over the decorative map — in the best sense of the phrase. Brandolini has created interiors that breezily juxtapose 18th-, 19th-, and 20th-century furnishings from every corner of the globe in rooms with vibrantly painted and upholstered walls ("Always the last thing I do," she notes). "I never approach a project with preconceived ideas," Brandolini adds. "I just do what I feel in the moment."

Muriel Brandolini hat seit ihrer Kindheit nicht mehr in Vietnam gelebt. Trotzdem hat die vietnamesisch-französisch-venezuelanische Innenarchitektin ihre südostasiatischen Wurzeln nicht vergessen. Ebenso wenig ihre internationale Herkunft – Brandolini lebte, bevor sie als junge Erwachsene in die Vereinigten Staaten zog, in Martinique und Frankreich. Kosmopolitisch ist auch ihr vierstöckiges Stadthaus aus den 1890ern, welches sie mit ihrem italienischen Ehemann Nuno, einem Banker, und ihren zwei Kindern an der Upper East Side bewohnt. Brandolinis Einrichtung ist eine unbekümmerte Melange verschiedenster Stilrichtungen aus aller Welt. Die Möbel stammen aus dem 18., 19. und 20. Jahrhundert, die Wände der Zimmer („ich gestalte sie immer zuletzt") sind bunt bemalt oder mit Stoff bezogen. „Meine Projekte gehe ich total unvoreingenommen an", sagt sie. „Ich mache immer das, was sich gerade richtig anfühlt."

Previous pages: *In the front hall, Michele Oka Doner's "Radiant Disk" table sits under a hand-embroidered silk lantern from Vietnam.*
Facing page: *Brandolini upholstered the study's pair of neoclassical banquettes in a mix of vintage Indian, Japanese, and French fabrics.*
Above: *A Ross Bleckner painting looks over the living room's eclectic furnishings, including Mattia Bonetti's "Smarties" cocktail table.*
Right: *In the master bedroom, an armchair upholstered in hand-embroidered fabric sits in front of a 1930s armoire.*

Pages précédentes : *Dans le hall d'entrée, « Radiant Disk », une table de Michele Oka Doner sous une lanterne vietnamienne en soie brodée.*
Page de gauche : *Brandolini a tapissé les deux banquettes néoclassiques de la bibliothèque d'un mélange de tissus anciens indiens, japonais et français.*
En haut : *Une toile de Ross Bleckner domine le séjour dont le mobilier éclectique inclut la table « Smarties » de Mattia Bonetti.*
À droite : *Dans la chambre des maîtres, un fauteuil tapissé d'une étoffe brodée devant une armoire des années 1930.*

Vorhergehende Seiten: *In der Eingangshalle: der monumentale Tisch „Radiant Disk" aus Gussbronze von Michele Oka Doner, unter einer Laterne aus Seidenstoff aus Vietnam.*
Gegenüberliegende Seite: *Brandolini ließ die beiden klassizistischen Sitzbänke mit Stoffen aus Indien, Japan und Frankreich beziehen.*
Oben: *Riesiges Bild von Ross Bleckner und eklektische Einrichtungsstücke wie der „Smarties"-Cocktailtisch von Mattia Bonetti.*
Rechts: *Im großen Schlafzimmer: ein mit handbesticktem Stoff bezogener Sessel, dahinter ein 1930er-Schrank.*

Above: The steel dining table by Martin Szekely is surrounded by 19th-century Louis XV-style chairs and a 1780s French settee; the walls are covered in Vietnamese hand-embroidered silk.
Right: On the other side of the dining room, pillows in vintage fabrics from China, Turkey, and Japan cover a 19th-century daybed.
Facing page: Ingo Maurer's "Zettel'z 5" light fixture hangs over the kitchen's massive 1940s marble table by Jean Dunand; the custom cabinets are faced in zinc.

En haut : La table de salle à manger en acier, de Martin Szekely, est entourée de chaises de style Louis XV du 19ᵉ siècle et d'une banquette française des années 1780 ; les murs sont tapissés d'une soie brodée vietnamienne.
À droite : À l'autre bout de la salle à manger, un lit du 19ᵉ siècle est recouvert de coussins en tissus anciens chinois, turcs et japonais.
Page de droite : Dans la cuisine, au-dessus d'une massive table en marbre des années 1940 de Jean Dunand, un plafonnier d'Ingo Maurer, « Zettel'z 5 ». Les placards sont recouverts de zinc.

Oben: Die Stühle im Louis-XV-Stil rund um den Stahl-Esstisch von Martin Szekely sind aus dem 19. Jahrhundert, die Sitzbank von 1780 kommt aus Frankreich. Die Wände sind mit handbestickter vietnamesischer Seide tapeziert.
Rechts: Auf dem Bettsofa aus dem 19. Jahrhundert auf der anderen Seite des Esszimmers sind die Kissen mit Vintage-Stoffen aus China, der Türkei und Japan bezogen.
Gegenüberliegende Seite: Die „Zettel'z 5"-Leuchte von Ingo Maurer über dem massiven Marmorküchentisch von Jean Dunand aus den 1940ern. Die mit Zink verkleideten Küchenschränke sind eine Spezialanfertigung.

Above: Framed works, including a Philip Taaffe painting, a Van Day Truex drawing, and 18th-century embroidered panels, surround the master bed.
Right: In daughter Filipa's bedroom, a "Muff Daddy" lounge chair by Jerszy Seymour sits near a 1950s Greta Magnusson Grossman desk.
Facing page: The ceiling of the media/guest room is covered with vintage Indian silk saris. A pair of 1905 painted armchairs and a 1960s coffee table by Philip and Kelvin LaVerne sit on a "Coral" rug by Fedora Design.

En haut : Le lit de la chambre principale, recouvert d'une étoffe du 18e siècle, est entouré d'œuvres encadrées, dont une peinture de Philip Taaffe et un dessin de Van Day Truex.
À droite : Dans la chambre de Filipa un fauteuil « Muff Daddy » de Jerszy Seymour et un bureau des années 1950 de Greta Magnusson Grossman.
Page de droite : Le plafond de la chambre d'ami est tapissé de saris en soie. La paire de fauteuils peints datant de 1905 et une table basse des années 1960 de Philip et Kelvin LaVerne sont sur un tapis « Coral » de Fedora Design.

Oben: Gerahmte Werke, darunter ein Bild von Philip Taaffe, eine Zeichnung von Van Day Truex und bestickte Paneele aus dem 18. Jahrhundert umrahmen das Bett.
Rechts: Im Zimmer von Tochter Filipa: ein „Muff Daddy"-Klubsessel von Jerszy Seymour und ein Schreibtisch aus den 1950ern von Greta Magnusson Grossman.
Gegenüberliegende Seite: Die Decke im Medien- und Gästezimmer ist mit indischen Vintage-Seidensaris bezogen. Zwei bemalte Sessel von 1905 neben einem 1960er-Klubtisch von Philip und Kelvin LaVerne. Auf dem Boden: der „Coral"-Teppich von Fedora Design.

New New York Interiors   Muriel Brandolini

La photographe Anita Calero s'est installée à West Chelsea bien avant la ruée des millionnaires, louant ce loft de 185 mètres carrées dans un immeuble d'artistes dans les années 1990, avant de l'acheter et de le réaménager. Elle a ouvert partout de grandes portes, notamment dans la cuisine dont l'équipement a été soigneusement dissimulé. Elle fait également office de salle à manger, avec une table et des chaises de Jean Prouvé et un lustre en faux corail. Calero aime chiner chez les antiquaires et aux puces. Les moulures en acajou et en frêne utilisées dans tout l'appartement s'accordent avec les sols en béton qui, une fois décapés, ont révélé des taches d'encre datant de l'époque où l'espace accueillait une imprimerie. Naturellement, ce type d'archéologie serait impossible dans les luxueux immeubles d'appartements qui s'élèvent partout dans le quartier. « Ils me bouchent de plus en plus la vue », soupire Calero.

Anita Calero

Photographer Anita Calero migrated to West Chelsea long before the current stampede of millionaires. Back in the 1990s, she rented a 2,000-square-foot loft in an artists' condominium, which she then bought and began to reconfigure. Calero knocked wide doorways into several rooms, including the new eat-in kitchen, its major appliances carefully hidden from the adjacent spaces. The dining table and chairs are lightly restored Jean Prouvé, with a faux-coral chandelier above – Calero frequents furniture dealers and flea markets. The mahogany and ash trim used throughout the apartment complements the concrete floors, which Calero stripped of paint to reveal ink stains from the era when printers worked in the loft. Of course, this kind of archaeology isn't possible in the ultra-luxury apartments rising around Calero's building. "I've been losing windows," she sighs.

Die Fotografin Anita Calero zog lange vor dem Ansturm der Millionäre nach West Chelsea. In den 1990ern mietete sie in einem Wohnhaus, in dem viele Künstler leben, ein 185 Quadratmeter großes Loft, das sie später kaufte und umbaute. Sie riss Wände ein und machte aus großzügigen Zimmerfluchten mit breiten Durchgängen mehrere kleine Räume, wie beispielsweise die neue Essküche, in der die großen Elektrogeräte so eingebaut sind, dass man sie nicht sieht. Über dem Esstisch und den Stühlen von Jean Prouvé, hängt ein Leuchter aus Korallen-Imitat, den Calero bei einer ihrer Streifzüge durch Möbelgalerien und Flohmärkte aufgestöbert hat. Die Mahagoni- und Eschenholzleisten, die sich durchs ganze Apartment ziehen, bilden eine schöne Ergänzung zu den kühlen Betonböden. Als Calero die Bodenfarbe auf den Betonböden ablaugte, kamen Tintenflecke aus der alten Druckereizeit des Lofts zum Vorschein. Solch charmante Überreste gibt's in den Superluxusapartments, die rund um Caleros Haus entstehen, nicht. Calero: „Aber meine Aussicht verschwindet langsam."

Left: The two sofas in the living room are by George Nakashima, while the tall wood cabinet in the background is by Jean Prouvé.
Below: On the wall behind the teak and red-leather Ib Kofod-Larsen chair is a realist painting of Lenin, found in a Moscow flea market, and a contemporary portrait by the New York artist James Brown.

À gauche : Dans le séjour, les deux canapés sont de George Nakashima. La haute armoire en bois au fond est de Jean Prouvé.
En bas : Posé contre le mur derrière le fauteuil en teck et cuir rouge d'Ib Kofod-Larsen, un portrait réaliste de Lénine trouvé sur un marché aux puces de Moscou. Sur la droite, un portrait contemporain de l'artiste new-yorkais James Brown.

Links: Die beiden Sofas im Wohnzimmer sind von George Nakashima. Der hohe Wandschrank im Hintergrund ist von Jean Prouvé.
Unten: Mit rotem Leder bezogener Teak-Stuhl von Ib Kofod-Larsen; an der Wand dahinter steht ein Bild in realistischer Malweise von Lenin – ein Fundstück von einem Moskauer Flohmarkt – neben einem zeitgenössischen Porträt des New Yorker Künstlers James Brown.

Previous pages: In the kitchen-dining room, a faux-coral chandelier hangs over lightly restored vintage table and chairs by Jean Prouvé.
Facing page: In the library, an industrial desk lamp stands beside a Jean Prouvé daybed, over which hangs a vintage Danish painted-aluminum light; beside the door, an Irving Penn print hangs on the wall above a Charlotte Perriand table.

Pages précédentes : Dans la cuisine/salle à manger, un lustre en imitation corail est suspendu au-dessus d'une table et de chaises de Jean Prouvé légèrement restaurées.
Page de gauche : Dans la bibliothèque, une lampe de bureau industrielle près d'un lit de repos de Jean Prouvé, sous un plafonnier danois vintage en aluminium peint. Près de la porte, une reproduction d'Irving Penn au-dessus d'une table de Charlotte Perriand.

Vorhergehende Seiten: Leuchter aus Korallen-Imitat über Vintage-Tisch und -Stühlen von Jean Prouvé in der Essküche. Die Vintage-Stücke wurden nur wenig restauriert.
Gegenüberliegende Seite: Industrie-Schreibtischlampe neben einer Liege von Jean Prouvé in der Bibliothek. Darüber hängt eine farbig lackierte dänische Aluminiumlampe. Über dem Tisch von Charlotte Perriand an der Wand neben der Tür hängt ein Fotoprint von Irving Penn.

Comme le savent les deux sommités de l'art qui occupent cet espace de 250 mètres carrés dominant Central Park, tout est dans la perspective. Ils ont échangé leur appartement traditionnel du Upper East Side contre ce skybox au-dessus de Columbus Circle. Comme le dit l'un deux, « vivre 66 étages au-dessus des soucis de la ville modifie votre sens esthétique et libère votre esprit ». Cela sert également de catalyseur à une architecture originale qui se reflète dans les formes irrégulières des pièces. Pour créer un lieu adapté à l'expérimentation esthétique et exhiber une collection basée sur les forces primaires de la vie, « éros » et « thanatos », ils ont tapissé le cœur de l'appartement de contreplaqué. « C'est un matériau de construction riche de possibilités. En outre, vous pouvez accrocher et décrocher des œuvres à loisir sans vous préoccuper des trous. »

Columbus Circle

Perspective is everything, as the two art-world luminaries occupying this 2,700-square-foot three-bedroom residence high above Central Park know well. The couple had been content in the traditional Upper East Side apartment they exchanged for a skybox over Columbus Circle. But, as one of them says, life at the top "changes your aesthetic expectations. Living 66 floors above the worries of the city liberates your mind." It's also a catalyst for unorthodox design, as the irregular spaces demonstrate. To create a place suited to aesthetic experimentation and the potential of making mistakes, and to show off an art collection focused on life's prime forces, "eros" and "thanatos," they lined the apartment's core in plywood. "That stage of construction is pregnant with possibilities," one owner says. "Plus, you can re-hang pictures, and holes don't matter."

Perspektive ist alles. Das wissen die beiden Größen der Kunstwelt, die diese über 250 Quadratmeter große Residenz mit drei Schlafzimmern hoch über dem Central Park bewohnen. Das Paar war zwar mit der traditionellen Wohnung, die es zuvor an der Upper East Side bewohnte, glücklich, dennoch lockte das Leben hoch über dem Columbus Circle. „In der 66. Etage schwebt man über den Sorgen und der Hektik dieser Stadt. Das ist befreiend für den Geist, und es verändert die Vorstellungen von Ästhetik", erklärt einer der Bewohner. Die luftige Höhe und unregelmäßig gewinkelte Wände scheinen auch zu ungewöhnlichem Design zu inspirieren. Das Kernstück des Apartments ist mit Sperrholz ausgekleidet – dies erlaubt visuelle Experimente und dient als Hintergrund für die Kunstsammlung der Bewohner rund um die Urkräfte „Eros" und „Thanatos". „Und das Umhängen und Rearrangieren der Bilder ist nach Belieben möglich, denn Löcher sind nicht weiter auffällig."

Previous pages: British art duo Tim Noble and Sue Webster' light-bulb dollar sign hangs in the entry. Columbus Circle at night, from the 66th floor. A Barry McGee wall installation above the striped carpet that's used throughout.
Above: In the library, a work by Adam McEwen leans against the bookshelves near a Jonathan Meese ceramic assemblage.
Right: Like many of the apartment's other rooms, the art library and office is an irregular shape.

Pages précédentes : Dans l'entrée, le dollar en ampoules lumineuses du duo artistique britannique Tim Noble et Sue Webster ; les murs sont tapissés de contreplaqué. Columbus Circle la nuit, vu du 66ᵉ étage. Une installation murale de Barry McGee ; la même moquette rayée est utilisée dans tout l'appartement.
En haut : Dans la bibliothèque, une œuvre d'Adam McEwen est posée contre les étagères, près d'un assemblage en céramique de Jonathan Meese.
À droite : Comme de nombreuses pièces de l'appartement, la biblio-thèque/bureau a une forme irrégulière.

Vorhergehende Seiten: Dollar-Zeichen aus Glühbirnen vom britischen Künstlerduo Tim Noble und Sue Webster im Eingangsbereich. Columbus Circle bei Nacht – Ausblick von der 66. Etage. Wand-installation von Barry McGee. Der gestreifte Teppich zieht sich durchs ganze Apartment.
Oben: In der Bibliothek lehnt eine Arbeit von Adam McEwen am Bücherregal neben einer Jonathan-Meese-Keramikassemblage.
Rechts: Kunstbibliothek und Büro haben – wie die meisten anderen Räume – unregelmäßig gewinkelte Wände.

Right: A large 1982 silk-screen of a gun by Andy Warhol dominates one end of the psychedelically colorful living room.
Below: At night, with the lighting in the living room low, the glass fourth wall turns into an extension of the dynamically patterned interior.

À droite : Dans un coin du séjour psychédélique, une grande sérigraphie d'Andy Warhol de 1982 représentant un revolver.
En bas : La nuit, avec les lumières tamisées, la vue à travers le mur en verre devient une extension du décor coloré et dynamique du séjour.

Rechts: Im psychedelisch bunten Wohnzimmer dominiert der große Siebdruck „Gun" von Andy Warhol von 1982.
Unten: Nachts, wenn die Beleuchtung im Wohnzimmer schummrig ist, wirkt die Aussicht durch die Glasfront wie eine Erweiterung des Interieurs.

Previous pages: Living room walls are covered in "Garden 5,"
a psychedelic wallpaper by artist Eli Sudbrack (a.k.a. assume vivid
astro focus). "Clairvoyant", a John Currin painting in an early
17th-century Florentine frame hangs over an 18th-century chest
topped by a Tony Duquette soapstone pagoda lamp.
Right: "Tom Cruising," the black-and-white mural in the master
bedroom, is also by assume vivid astro focus.
Below: A Ron Arad chair and two 1970s chromed-metal wall sconces
(lamps) by Maria Pergay for Pierre Cardin add reflective surfaces
to the room.

Pages précédentes : Les murs du séjour sont tapissés de
« Garden 5 », un papier peint psychédélique d'Eli Sudbrack (alias
assume vivid astro focus). « Clairvoyant », de John Currin, dans un
cadre florentin du début du 17ᵉ siècle, est accroché au-dessus d'une
commode du 18ᵉ siècle sur laquelle est posée une lampe pagode en
stéatite de Tony Duquette.
À droite : « Tom Cruising », la peinture murale noire et blanche dans
la chambre des maîtres, est également d'assume vivid astro focus.
En bas : Un fauteuil de Ron Arad et des appliques chromées de Maria
Pergay pour Pierre Cardin ajoutent un effet miroir dans la chambre.

Vorhergehende Seiten: Die psychedelische Tapete „Garden 5" an
den Wohnzimmerwänden wurde vom Künstler Eli Sudbrack (auch
bekannt als assume vivid astro focus) entworfen. Eine Pagodenlampe
aus Speckstein von Tony Duquette steht auf einer Kommode aus dem
18. Jahrhundert. Darüber hängt in einem florentinischen Rahmen aus
dem frühen 17. Jahrhundert das Bild „Clairvoyant" von John Currin.
Rechts: Die schwarz-weiße Wandarbeit „Tom Cruising" im Schlafzimmer stammt ebenfalls von assume vivid astro focus.
Unten: Ein Stuhl von Ron Arad und zwei verchromte Lampen aus
den 1970ern von Maria Pergay für Pierre Cardin bieten Reflektions-
flächen im Schlafzimmer.

Above: A 19th-century Chinese daybed with a Huanuco fur cover
dominates the media room. The chair is by Chicago architect
Ron Krueck.
Right: A sculpture by Dan Colen in a corner of the master bedroom.
Following pages: The light-bulb dollar sign is reflected in the living
room window, an amusing comment on the nighttime Manhattan
skyline beyond.

En haut : Un lit chinois du 19ᵉ siècle, avec un dessus-de-lit en fourrure
provenant de Huanuco, domine la médiathèque. Le fauteuil est de
l'architecte Ron Krueck, originaire de Chicago.
À droite : Dans un coin de la chambre principale, une sculpture
de Dan Colen.
Pages suivantes : Le symbole du dollar se reflète dans la vitre
du séjour, offrant un commentaire amusant sur la vue nocturne de
Manhattan.

Oben: Ein chinesisches Liegesofa aus dem 19. Jahrhundert mit einem
Überwurf aus Huanuco-Fell ist ein Blickfang im Medienzimmer.
Der Stuhl ist ein Entwurf des Chicagoer Architekten Ron Krueck.
Rechts: Kunst im Schlafzimmer: Skulptur von Dan Colen.
Folgende Seiten: Im Fenster des Wohnzimmers spiegelt sich das
Dollar-Zeichen aus Glühbirnen: eine augenzwinkernde Referenz an
die nächtliche Skyline von Manhattan.

Quand le styliste capillaire Gerald DeCock y a emménagé en 1994, cet appartement atelier du Chelsea Hotel était tout blanc. À présent, le moindre recoin des 75 mètres carrés est une explosion de couleurs étourdissante. Après avoir enduit d'une couche de peinture acrylique murs, sols et plafonds, il y a appliqué toutes sortes de matières hétéroclites, en commençant par les murs en briques qu'il a recouverts de feuilles d'or, puis laqués, peints en rouge japonais et enfin badigeonnés de vernis sombre pour bois pour obtenir un effet de brûlé. Ce n'était que le début de ses expériences décoratives qui confèrent désormais à chaque couleur et texture la complexité d'une œuvre d'art. Il n'y a donc rien d'étonnant à ce que, une fois à court de surface à barbouiller, il se soit attaqué à des toiles de peintre.

Gerald DeCock

When hairstylist Gerald DeCock moved into his Chelsea Hotel studio apartment in 1994, it was completely white. Now every surface in the 800-square-foot space has been transfigured into a slab of richly layered color. Not content to slap on a coat of acrylic paint, DeCock has applied a dazzling, if unorthodox, array of materials to his walls, floors, and ceilings. Take the brick wall he began with: First he covered it with gold leaf; then he applied a coat of shellac, followed by one of Japan Red paint; and he finished it off with dark wood stain for a burnt effect. This was the first in an ongoing series of decorative experiments, with the result that the colour and texture of the apartment's surfaces now have the complexity of works of art. So it's not surprising that when he ran out of walls to daub, DeCock took up painting on canvas like a regular artist.

Als Hairstylist Gerald DeCock 1994 in dieses Studio-Apartment im Chelsea Hotel zog, war es ganz weiß. Heute ist jede Oberfläche des 75 Quadratmeter großen Raums mit dicken Farbschichten belegt. Einfach nur eine Acrylfarbe auftragen und fertig – das ist nicht DeCocks Sache. Lieber spielt er mit einer schillernden, unorthodoxen Vielfalt an Materialien und appliziert sie auf Wände, Böden und Decken. Nach dem Einzug machte er sich als Erstes an die Backsteinwand: zuerst eine Schicht Blattgold, dann eine Schicht Schellack, darüber noch eine Schicht Farbe in Japanrot, und zum Schluss rundete er sein Werk mit dunkler Holzbeize ab, um einen Effekt von Angebranntem zu erzeugen. Das Resultat spornte DeCock zu weiteren dekorativen Experimenten an. Die Farben und Strukturen der Oberflächen in seinem Apartment sind so komplex wie ein Kunstwerk. So ist es nicht überraschend, dass DeCock, der keine freien Wände mehr zur Verfügung hat, nun Leinwände bemalt – wie ein richtiger Künstler.

Previous pages: *A friend made the glittery vinyl beanbag for DeCock.*
Facing Page: *The brick wall was the first surface DeCock decorated. He spray-painted the sofa red, and covered gold leaf and glittery contact paper with a sheet of plastic to create the top of the coffee table.*
Above: *The living room floor is stained orange. Curtains of plastic Mardi Gras beads hang between the kitchen and the living room.*
Right: *The ladder in the kitchen leads to the roof terrace.*

Pages précédentes : *Un ami de DeCock lui a réalisé le sacco en vinyle brillant.*
Page de gauche : *Le mur en briques a été le premier auquel DeCock s'est attaqué. Le canapé rouge a été peint à la bombe. La table basse a été recouverte de feuilles d'or et de papier contact brillant avant d'être enduite d'une couche de plastique.*
En haut : *Le sol du séjour a été teint en orange. La cuisine et le séjour sont séparés par des rideaux réalisés avec des perles en plastique que l'on se jette à la Nouvelle-Orléans durant Mardi Gras.*
À droite : *L'échelle dans la cuisine mène à la terrasse sur le toit.*

Vorhergehende Seiten: *Den glänzenden Vinyl-Sitzsack hat ein Freund für DeCock entworfen.*
Gegenüberliegende Seite: *Diese Backsteinwand verschönte DeCock als Erstes. Das Sofa besprühte er mit roter Farbe. Auf die Couchtischplatte klebte er Blattgold, glitzerndes Kontaktpapier und Plastikfolie.*
Oben: *Der Wohnzimmerboden ist orangefarben gebeizt. Die Vorhänge zwischen Küche und Wohnzimmer sind aus „Mardi Gras"-Plastikperlenketten.*
Rechts: *Die Leiter in der Küche führt auf die Dachterrasse.*

Vanessa del Rio

A small mermaid in the front garden is the only sign that a suburban house on Staten Island belongs to Vanessa del Rio, the retired porn actress who became the first Latina superstar in American adult films during the 1970s and 1980s. Inside, however, del Rio's home is an unfettered expression of her buoyant personality. "I love anything tropical," she says, as the fabrics and rugs patterned with lush jungle foliage and animal prints attest. There's also a pronounced Asian motif, as well as a passion for gilding, "which I probably got from my mother," she says with a laugh. "Her way of freshening up the house was to apply gold paint." Chicago decorative artist Meridee Hodges gave the walls and ceilings a variety of faux finishes, including fresco, gold leaf, decoupage, and Venetian plaster. That apart, del Rio did all the decorating, using a simple principle: "Whatever I like, I collect."

Previous pages: A tropical scene on fabric hangs in the master bedroom.
Above: Del Rio's French bulldog, Matilda, stretches out on the living room's leopard-patterned carpet. In the windows, framed prints hang over matchstick blinds to provide privacy.
Right: A poster of Isabel Sarli, the Argentine movie star and sex symbol, who was one of del Rio's earliest inspirations.
Facing page: Buddha heads and other East Asian objects fill a glass-topped console in the dining area.

Pages précédentes : Dans la chambre principale, une tenture imprimée d'une scène tropicale.
En haut : Dans le salon, Matilda, un bouledogue français, s'étire sur le tapis en fausse peau de léopard. Des lithogravures encadrées sont accrochées aux stores devant les fenêtres pour assurer plus d'intimité.
À droite : Une affiche d'Isabel Sarli, star de cinéma argentine et sex-symbol, l'une des premières inspirations de del Rio.
Page de droite : Dans le coin repas, sur une console avec un plateau en verre, des têtes de bouddha et d'autres objets d'Extrême-Orient.

Vorherige Seiten: Eine Stoffbahn mit Tropenmotiv an der Schlafzimmerwand.
Oben: Auf dem Teppich mit Leopardenmuster im Wohnzimmer streckt sich Matilda, del Rios französische Bulldogge. Zwischen den Vorhängen, die für Privatsphäre sorgen, hängen gerahmte Bilddrucke.
Rechts: Das Poster zeigt die Schauspielerin Isabel Sarli. Das argentinische Sexsymbol war eines der frühen Vorbilder del Rios.
Gegenüberliegende Seite: Buddha-Köpfe und andere ostasiatische Objekte auf der Glasplatte der Konsole im Esszimmer.

New New York Interiors   Vanessa del Rio

Facing page: The Chicago decorative artist, Meridee Hodges, painted the zebra-patterned ceiling in the upstairs guest room. The photograph is of del Rio in the 1980s.
Following pages: Vignettes include a mannequin leg and head; a Thai parasol over the head of a temple dancer; a circus banner depicting a snake charmer draped with a python; and an alligator lurking under a chaise. Meridee Hodges applied gold leaf, which she then aged. Among the knickknacks on the bedroom bureau is a blue crystal ball, a good-luck gift that del Rio has kept for more than 30 years.

Page de droite : Meridee Hodges, une peintre décoratrice ornemaniste de Chicago, a peint le plafond de la chambre d'ami à l'étage en peau de zèbre. Posée sur le sol, une photo de del Rio des années 1980.
Pages suivantes : Une tête et une jambe de mannequin ; un parasol thaïlandais au-dessus d'une tête de danseuse sacrée ; une affiche de cirque représentant une charmeuse de serpent drapée dans un python ; un alligator tapi sous un lit de repos. Dans la chambre principale, Meridee Hodges a doré le plafond à la feuille avant de le patiner. Parmi les bibelots sur la commode, une boule en cristal bleu, un cadeau porte-bonheur que del Rio conserve depuis plus de trente ans.

Gegenüberliegende Seite: Die Kunsthandwerkerin Meridee Hodges aus Chicago malte im oberen Gästezimmer ein Zebramuster an die Decke. Das Foto am Boden zeigt del Rio in den 1980ern.
Folgende Seiten: Bein und Kopf von Schaufensterpuppen; ein thailändischer Sonnenschirm über dem Kopf einer Tempeltänzerin; Zirkusbanner mit pythonbehangener Schlangenbeschwörerin; ein Krokodil versteckt unter der Liege. Auf alt gemachte Goldblatt-Applikation von Meridee Hodges an der Decke des Schlafzimmers. Unter den Nippes auf der Schlafzimmerkommode steht eine blaue Kristallkugel. Der Glücksbringer ist ein Geschenk, das del Rio seit über 30 Jahren aufbewahrt.

Previous pages: A 1950s leopard-skin swing coat hangs on the back of a chair occupied by del Rio's cat, Tarzan. A porcelain tiger menaces a group of erotic Chinese figurines.
Above: Del Rio's collection of stiletto shoes ("These are just my sexy high heels," she says) is arrayed on shelves above wicker storage boxes in the dressing room.
Right: Wigs that del Rio uses on photo shoots are displayed on mannequin heads surrounding the circular mirror on her vanity table.

Pages précédentes : Un manteau trapèze en léopard posé sur le dossier d'une chaise occupée par Tarzan, le chat de la maison. Un tigre en porcelaine menace un groupe de figurines érotiques chinoises.
En haut : Dans le dressing, la collection de talons aiguilles de del Rio (« Ce ne sont que mes souliers les plus sexy ») est disposée au-dessus de boîtes de rangement en osier.
À droite : Les perruques que del Rio utilise pour ses prises de vue sont rangées sur des têtes de mannequin de chaque côté du miroir rond au-dessus de sa coiffeuse.

Vorhergehende Seiten: Del Rios Katze Tarzan liegt auf dem Stuhl, auf dessen Lehne ein Cape-Mantel im Leopardenmuster aus den 1950ern hängt. Ein fauchender Porzellantiger vor einer Gruppe chinesischer Erotikfiguren.
Oben: In den Wandregalen im Ankleidezimmer ist del Rios Stiletto-Sammlung säuberlich aufgereiht, „das sind nur meine sexy High Heels", sagt sie.
Rechts: Die Perücken auf den Schaufensterpuppenköpfen neben dem runden Spiegel auf dem Schminktisch trägt del Rio jeweils bei Fotoaufnahmen.

L'architecte Annabelle Selldorf, qui a dirigé la rénovation de cette maison en grès brun dans le East Village, ne tarit pas d'éloges sur ses clients, un couple cosmopolite : « Ce fut une collaboration parfaite entre nous trois. » Il est dans l'art, elle dans la mode, et ce sont de vieux amis. Le bâtiment était délabré mais possédait d'excellentes bases. « C'était une carcasse vide que nous avons remplie. » Une grande cuisine chaleureuse a été aménagée où la femme, cordon bleu, peut régaler leurs trois enfants. Les cinq étages sont reliés par un escalier central, couronné d'une verrière qui illumine le cœur de la maison. La demeure sert également de vitrine à une collection d'art contemporain. « Quand on conçoit un espace pour l'art, confie Selldorf, la clef est de créer des pièces aux belles proportions. »

An East Village Townhouse

Architect Annabelle Selldorf, who masterminded the renovation of this East Village brownstone, is quick to praise her clients: "It was a complete collaboration between the three of us," she says of the cosmopolitan couple – he's in the art world, she's in fashion – who are also her old friends. The wife found the townhouse, a wreck which Selldorf stripped bare. "It was an empty shell that we refilled," she says. The wife is a fine cook, so the kitchen is a large, warm space where her three children can gather. The five floors are connected by a central staircase, topped by a skylight so the core of the house is illuminated. The brownstone is also a showcase for a contemporary art collection. "We managed to create beautifully proportioned rooms," Selldorf says. "That's the secret to designing for art."

Architektin Annabelle Selldorf, der kreative Kopf der gelungenen Renovierung dieses Backsteinhauses im East Village, teilt den Erfolg mit ihren Kunden, einem kosmopolitischen Paar, mit dem sie seit Langem befreundet ist – er ist aus der Kunstszene, sie in der Modewelt. „Es war ein Zusammenspiel von uns dreien", sagt sie. Die Hausherrin hatte das Stadthaus gefunden, das zwar heruntergekommen war, aber eine gute Grundstruktur besaß. Selldorf befreite es von allem Überflüssigen: „Dadurch konnten wir Neues schaffen." Die Küche ist groß und passt zur Besitzerin, eine Gourmetköchin. Hier halten sich auch ihre drei Kinder gerne auf. Die fünf Etagen des Hauses sind mit einer eleganten Treppe verbunden; zuoberst befindet sich ein Oberlicht, das das Innere des Hauses mit Licht erfüllt. Auch die bedeutende Sammlung zeitgenössischer Kunst der Eigentümer hat in dem Haus Platz: „Wir haben es geschafft, die Räume optimal zu proportionieren", sagt Selldorf, „das ist das Geheimnis, eine Kunstsammlung gut zur Geltung zu bringen."

Previous pages: In the formal living room, a portrait by Francis Picabia, flanked by works by On Kawara, hangs over an English mantelpiece.
Above: The formal dining room is on the second floor; the airy library can be seen beyond.
Right: Selldorf designed an elegantly austere central staircase for the brownstone; she topped the stairwell with a new skylight that allows daylight into the core of the house.

Pages précédentes : Dans le grand salon, un portrait de Francis Picabia trône au-dessus de la cheminée anglaise, flanquée d'œuvres de On Kawara.
En haut : La salle à manger se trouve au premier étage. Derrière, on aperçoit la lumineuse bibliothèque.
À droite : Selldorf a dessiné l'élégant et austère escalier central. Une nouvelle verrière au-dessus laisse entrer la lumière du jour jusqu'au cœur de la maison.

Vorhergehende Seiten: Über dem Sims des englischen Kamins im Wohnzimmer hängt ein Porträt von Francis Picabia zwischen Werken von On Kawara.
Oben: Das Esszimmer befindet sich in der zweiten Etage; von hier sieht man hinüber in die geräumige Bibliothek.
Rechts: Selldorf entwarf die streng-elegante Treppe in der Mitte des Backsteinhauses. Darüber hat sie ein Oberlicht einbauen lassen, damit Tageslicht ins Innere des Hauses gelangt.

Right: The light and airy library/living room is at the front of the house.
Below: The ground-floor kitchen was conceived as a welcoming room for family and friends. Artist Paula Hayes landscaped the back garden.
Following pages: The formal living room enjoys superb light from the new steel-and-glass French doors that overlook the back garden.

À droite : Le séjour/bibliothèque, clair et spacieux, se trouve sur le devant de la maison.
En bas : Au rez-de-chaussée, la cuisine, avec son sol au ton chaud, a été conçue pour accueillir la famille et les amis. L'artiste et paysagiste Paula Hayes a aménagé le jardin derrière la maison.
Pages suivantes : Grâce aux nouvelles portes-fenêtres en acier qui dominent le jardin, le grand salon est inondé d'une belle lumière.

Rechts: Der luftig-großzügige Wohnraum mit Bibliothek liegt an der Frontseite des Hauses.
Unten: Die Küche im Erdgeschoss wurde als Empfangsraum für Familie und Freunde konzipiert. Die Künstlerin Paula Hayes gestaltete den Garten hinter dem Haus.
Folgende Seiten: Helles Licht fällt durch die neuen stahlgerahmten Fenstertüren in das große Wohnzimmer; sie führen in den Garten hinter dem Haus.

Above: The walls of the casual family area, with its relaxing corner daybed, are festooned with colorful drawings by Raymond Pettibon.
Right: The dining chairs, covered in vivid African prints, are by the artist Franz West. The wall-size line drawing of a chain-link fence is by Toba Khedoori.

En haut : Les murs du petit coin familial, avec son lit de repos en angle, sont tapissés de dessins colorés de Raymond Pettibon.
À droite : Les chaises de la salle à manger, tapissées de tissus africains vivement colorés, sont de l'artiste Franz West. Le dessin d'un volume grillagé, qui occupe tout un mur, est de Toba Khedoori.

Oben: Die Wände des Familienzimmers sind mit farbigen Zeichnungen von Raymond Pettibon geschmückt. Eine Eckliege lädt zur Entspannung ein.
Rechts: Esstischstühle des Künstlers Franz West mit fröhlich gemusterten afrikanischen Stoffen; die wandgroße Zeichnung eines Maschendrahtzauns stammt von Toba Khedoori.

Right: A Gerhard Richter hangs above the master bed; twin pedestal sinks in the master bathroom.
Below: The master bathroom, which occupies the full width of the front of the house, has marble walls, a wooden cold tub, sauna, and freestanding bathtub. The floor is the same oiled wide-plank oak used throughout the house.

À droite : Dans la chambre des maîtres, un Gerhard Richter est accroché au-dessus du lit. Dans la salle de bain principale, deux lavabos jumeaux.
En bas : La salle de bain principale, située à l'avant de la maison, occupe toute sa largeur et possède des murs en marbre. Elle est équipée d'un baquet d'eau froide, d'un sauna et d'une baignoire sur pied. Le sol est en parquet de chêne huilé à larges lattes comme le reste de la maison.

Rechts: Im großen Schlafzimmer hängt ein Werk von Gerhard Richter über dem Bett; das Bad verfügt über zwei Waschbecken auf Säulenfüßen.
Unten: Das große Badezimmer mit marmorverkleideten Wänden zieht sich über die ganze Länge des vorderen Hausteils. Es ist mit einem Kaltwasserzuber aus Holz, einer Sauna und einer frei stehenden Badewanne ausgestattet. Wie im ganzen Haus ist der Boden aus geölten breiten Eichendielen.

Left: The younger daughter's bedroom has large steel-frame French doors – an acknowledgement that this is may be a modern house, but it has a history – which overlook the rear garden.
Below: With its canopied bed, the elder daughter's bedroom strikes a note of overt romanticism.

À gauche : La maison a beau être moderne, elle a aussi un passé. La chambre de la benjamine est équipée de hautes portes-fenêtres qui donnent sur le jardin.
En bas : Avec son lit à baldaquin, la chambre de l'aînée est romantique à souhait.

Links: Die großen stahlgerahmten Glastüren im Schlafzimmer der jüngeren Tochter sind genauso modern wie historisch. Durch sie sieht man auf den hinteren Garten.
Unten: Das Zimmer der älteren Tochter ist etwas romantischer – es hat ein Himmelbett.

Facing page: Simple slip-covered sofas and an Eero Saarinen "Tulip" coffee table put an emphasis on comfort and ease in the library, which faces the street. The beautifully proportioned room takes full advantage of the brownstone's generous ceiling heights.

Page de gauche : La bibliothèque, avec ses canapés recouverts d'une simple housse blanche et sa table basse « Tulip » d'Eero Saarinen, met l'accent sur le confort. Donnant sur la rue, ses belles proportions profitent au maximum de la généreuse hauteur sous plafond.

Gegenüberliegende Seite: Einfache mit Hussen überzogene Sofas und ein „Tulip"-Couchtisch von Eero Saarinen betonen die komfortable, entspannte Atmosphäre in der Bibliothek. Von hier sieht man auf die Straße. Die schön proportionierten Räume nutzen die großzügige Zimmerhöhe.

Le penthouse du photographe Pieter Estersohn à Gramercy Park a presque tout ce qu'il souhaitait pour sa demeure new-yorkaise, ainsi qu'une histoire intéressante. Ajouté dans les années 1920 à un immeuble construit en 1903, il appartenait autrefois à l'auteur et illustrateur Ludwig Bemelmans. En outre, il s'accompagnait de la clef très convoitée du seul parc privé de Manhattan. Il a abattu des murs, percé une verrière et créé l'atelier dont il rêvait depuis qu'il avait quitté Paris des années plus tôt. À la naissance de son fils, il a acheté l'appartement du dessous pour obtenir un duplex de 150 mètres carrés avec deux chambres et deux salles de bain. Le décor mélange l'ancien et le moderne, et sans être « trop sophistiqué », jouit d'une belle patine. Voyageur infatigable, Estersohn y a rassemblé des objets du monde entier. Le seul inconvénient ? « Je manque de surface d'accrochage, c'est un peu frustrant », dit-il.

Pieter Estersohn

Photographer Pieter Estersohn's apartment on Gramercy Park has almost everything he wanted in a Manhattan home – and some interesting history. Estersohn's penthouse, added to the 1903 building in the 1920s, once belonged to the author and illustrator Ludwig Bemelmans. And the place came with a coveted key to the city's only private park. Estersohn gutted the interior, put in a skylight, and created the atelier he'd wanted since living in Paris years ago. Later, with the birth of his son imminent, he acquired the apartment below to create a 1,600-square-foot two-bedroom, two-bath residence. The interiors are a mix of old and new, "not too polished," says Estersohn, but with a lovely patina. An inveterate traveler, he's furnished the place with pieces collected from all over the world. The one drawback? "Limited wall space," he says. "It's a bit frustrating."

Der Fotograf Pieter Estersohn kann sich kein besseres Zuhause in Manhattan vorstellen als dieses Apartment am Gramercy Park. Es hat auch noch eine interessante Geschichte aufzuweisen: Das Penthouse wurde in den 1920ern nachträglich auf das Haus aus dem Jahr 1903 gebaut und gehörte dem Autor und Illustrator Ludwig Bemelmans. Die Wohnung hat einen Zugangsschlüssel zum Gramercy Park, dem einzigen Privatpark der Stadt. Estersohn entkernte sein neues Zuhause, ließ ein Oberlicht einbauen und richtete sich so eine Atelierwohnung ein, wie er es sich seit seiner Pariser Zeit erträumte. Vor der Geburt seines Sohnes kaufte er noch die Wohnung in der unteren Etage: zusätzliche 150 Quadratmeter mit zwei Schlaf- und zwei Badezimmern. Die Einrichtung ist eine Melange aus Alt und Neu, „nicht zu gepützelt, dafür mit Patina" und voller Stücke, die der Vielgereiste aus aller Welt mitgebracht hat. „Einziger Wehrmutstropfen", sagt der Hausherr, „sind die knappen Wandflächen."

Previous pages: Estersohn uses the long hallway as a gallery for photographs and paintings by both his mother and himself.
Above: The daybed in the living area is by Jean Prouvé. A 19th-century Egyptian frame on an easel from the École des Beaux-Arts in Paris.
Right: The renovation revealed the original beam-and-channel ceiling.
Facing page: The cabinet over the kitchen sink is by Charlotte Perriand and Jean Prouvé. Estersohn purchased the French 19th-century dining chairs when he was 20, and covered them in cowhide.

Pages précédentes : Le long couloir sert de galerie pour les photographies et les tableaux d'Estersohn et de sa mère.
En haut : Dans le séjour, un lit de repos de Jean Prouvé. Au fond, un cadre égyptien du 19ᵉ siècle, posé sur un chevalet provenant de l'École des Beaux-Arts de Paris.
À droite : Les travaux ont dévoilé le plafond en cannelures et poutrelles apparentes datant des années 1920.
Page de droite : Le placard au-dessus de l'évier est de Charlotte Perriand et de Jean Prouvé. Estersohn a acheté les chaises de salle à manger, datant du 19ᵉ siècle, il les a tapissées de peau de vache.

Vorhergehende Seiten: Der lange Flur wurde zur Foto- und Gemäldegalerie umfunktioniert. Alle Werke sind von Estersohn und seiner Mutter.
Oben: Die Liege im Wohnzimmer ist von Jean Prouvé. Der Rahmen im Hintergrund stammt aus Ägypten, ist aus dem 19. Jahrhundert und steht auf einer Staffelei aus der École des Beaux-Arts in Paris.
Rechts: Bei der Renovierung wurde die gewölbte Decke mit Dachbalken aus den 1920ern freigelegt.
Gegenüberliegende Seite: Der Hängeschrank an der Küchenwand ist von Charlotte Perriand und Jean Prouvé. Die französischen Stühle aus dem 19. Jahrhundert entdeckte Estersohn, als er 20 war, und ließ sie mit Kuhfell beziehen.

Previous pages: Egyptian and Turkish lamps hang from the 15-foot high skylight. A sculptor friend carved the Brancusi-inspired book-cases. The leather-and-metal armchair is Jacques Adnet.
Facing page: Estersohn enlarged his own photographs of palace interiors in Rajasthan to paper the walls of his son's bedroom.
Above: The travertine-lined office and gallery space, connected by a spiral stair to the living room, has floors of 200-year-old white oak.
Right: The bathroom sink is a traditional Turkish sink.

Pages précédentes : Des lampes égyptiennes et turques, pendent de la verrière haute de 4,5 mètres. La bibliothèque en bois brut inspirée par Brancusi a été réalisée par un ami sculpteur il y a de longues années. Le fauteuil en cuir et métal est de Jacques Adnet.
Page de gauche : Pour tapisser les murs de la chambre de son fils, Estersohn a agrandi ses propres photos d'un palais du Rajasthan.
En haut : Au pied de l'escalier, un coin bureau et galerie a été tapissé de travertin. Les marches sont en chêne blanc de Virginie vieux de deux cents ans.
À droite : Le lavabo de la salle de bain est un ancien lavabo turc.

Vorhergehende Seiten: Ägyptische und türkische Lampen aus dem 17. bis 19. Jahrhundert im 4,5 Meter tiefen Oberlicht. Die von Brancusi inspirierten Bücherregale wurden von einem befreundeten Bildhauer geschnitzt. Der Sessel aus Metall und Leder ist von Jacques Adnet.
Gegenüberliegende Seite: Estersohns Fotografien von Innenräumen eines Palastes in Rajasthan dienten als Vorlage für die Tapeten im Schlafzimmer seines Sohnes.
Oben: Eine Treppe mit 200-jährigem weißen Eichenholz aus Virginia belegt, führt vom Wohnzimmer aus nach unten. Büro- und Galerie-wände sind beide mit Travertin verkleidet.
Rechts: Das Waschbecken ist ein traditionelles türkisches Becken.

Rénové il y a quarante ans par l'architecte Paul Rudolph, aujourd'hui disparu, cet appartement de 500 mètres carrés est comme une fenêtre temporelle sur le design d'avant-garde des années 1970. La propriétaire a conservé les pièces principales telles que Rudolph les avait conçues : avec leurs plates-formes courbes, leurs plafonds ornementés, leur éclairage innovateur, la disposition particulière des collections d'art et d'objets. Dans la salle à manger, un mur de niches rondes éclairées abrite des chinoiseries bleues et blanches. Dans le séjour, d'étroites bandes de miroirs sur le socle du sofa encastré semblent le faire léviter. Dans le bureau, d'autres bandes de miroir irradient d'une œuvre de Jean Arp collée au plafond, tandis que de minuscules miroirs de dentiste forment un motif décoratif sur les placards de la cuisine. La maîtresse des lieux est toujours aussi enthousiaste : « Rudolph avait un sens des matières inouï. Il était brillant ».

A Fifth Avenue Apartment

Remodeled four decades ago by the late architect Paul Rudolph, this 5,000-square-foot apartment is a time capsule of avant-garde 1970s design. The owner has preserved the major rooms exactly as Rudolph created them. That means curving floor platforms, complex ceiling treatments, innovative lighting, and idiosyncratically installed art and collectibles. A display wall in the dining room is a honeycomb of lighted circular niches holding pieces of blue-and-white china. In the living room, Rudolph applied narrow strips of mirror to the base of a built-in sofa so that it seems to levitate. More mirror strips radiate from a Jean Arp work on the office ceiling, while tiny round dentist's mirrors form decorative graphics on the kitchen cupboards. "The man's brilliance was so clear," says the delighted owner.

Vor vier Dekaden gestaltete der Architekt Paul Rudolph dieses fast 500 Quadratmeter große Apartment in reinem Avantgarde-Design der 1970er. Die heutige Besitzerin hat fast alle Räume im Originalzustand belassen, mit den geschwungenen Bodenplattformen, komplexen Deckengestaltungen, innovativen Beleuchtungen und ungewöhnlich installierten Kunst- und Sammlerobjekten. So sieht eine Wand im Esszimmer aus wie eine Bienenwabe: In einzeln beleuchteten runden Nischen werden blau-weiße Porzellanobjekte zur Schau gestellt. Und weil Rudolph den unteren Teil des Einbausofas im Wohnzimmer mit schmalen Spiegelstreifen versehen hat, sieht es aus, als würde es schweben. Im Arbeitszimmer glitzern rund um eine Arbeit von Hans Arp an der Decke schmale Spiegelstreifen. Und auf den Küchenschränken blitzen kleine, runde Zahnarztspiegel. „Die Brillanz des Mannes ist einfach sichtbar", sagt die hocherfreute Eigentümerin.

Left: A hallway serves as the art gallery for lithographs.
Below: The bed is built into a master bedroom alcove.
Facing page: The office ceiling boasts a Jean Arp sculpture within a sunburst of mirrors by Rudolph.

À gauche : Un couloir accueille une collection de lithographies.
En bas : Dans la chambre principale, le lit est encastré dans une alcôve.
Page de droite : Sur le plafond du bureau, Rudolph a créé un rayonnement de miroirs autour d'une sculpture de Jean Arp.

Links: Der Flur dient als Galerie, hier hängt eine ganze Reihe von Lithografien.
Unten: Das Bett im Schlafzimmer ist in einem Alkoven eingebaut.
Gegenüberliegende Seite: An der Bürodecke prangt ein Werk von Hans Arp mitten in der Spiegelstrahlenkreation von Rudolph.

Previous pages: Rudolph applied mirror-strips like tiles to curving walls. The living room includes Dutch paintings in elaborately gilded frames and, in the corner, an important construction by Larry Rivers. The ceramics collection is also displayed on bedroom shelves. Beneath a ceiling-mount starburst chandelier, the dining table is modular. Russian matryoshkas line the kitchen counter under cabinet doors emblazoned with decorative graphics made of round dentist's mirrors. Extra table modules are stowed beneath dining room display niches.

Pages précédentes : Rudolph a tapissé le bas des murs de bandelettes de miroirs. Dans le salon, des tableaux hollandais dans des cadres dorés ouvragés côtoient une sculpture polychrome de Larry Rivers. La collection de porcelaines se poursuit sur les étagères de la chambre. Dans la salle à manger, sous un plafonnier adial, une table modulaire. Sur le comptoir de la cuisine, des matriochkas russes devant des portes de placards décorés de petits miroirs de dentiste. Dans la salle à manger, les modules supplémentaires de la table s'encastrent sous le mur de niches.

Vorhergehende Seiten: Rudolph applizierte schmale Spiegelstreifen fliesenartig auf die geschwungenen Wände. Im Wohnzimmer hängen altniederländische Gemälde in kunstvoll geschnitzten goldenen Rahmen. In der Ecke steht eine Installation von Larry Rivers. Die blau-weiße Keramiksammlung hat auch auf den Regalen im Schlafzimmer Platz gefunden. An der Decke über dem modularen Esstisch ist ein strahlenförmiger Leuchter installiert. In der Küche zieren russische Matroschkas die Ablage unter den Schränken, die dekorativ mit runden Zahnarztspiegeln verschönt wurden. Unter der Nischenwand im Esszimmer finden Beistelltische Platz.

Copropriétaire de la galerie d'art Haas & Fuchs à Berlin, Michael Fuchs a ouvert une succursale à New York en 2006. Depuis, il vit entre les deux villes. À Manhattan, il a choisi un penthouse à Chelsea avec une terrasse panoramique et des vues imprenables. Il l'a aménagé simplement avec certains des meubles modernistes qu'il a accumulés au fil des ans (il a un faible pour Verner Panton, Hans Wegner et Alvar Aalto) et des pièces de son excellente collection d'art. « Nero's Pizza Oven » (2007), d'Eric Wesley, a trouvé sa place sur la terrasse tandis que « Roswitha » (2003), une sculpture en bois et pierre de Manfred Pernice, se dresse près de la cheminée. Dans la chambre, des tableaux de la seconde moitié du 20e siècle côtoient quatre œuvres de Giambattista Tiepolo récemment achetées. Fuchs déclare en riant : « Depuis peu, je m'intéresse aux dessins des grands maîtres. L'art contemporain est devenu trop cher. »

Michael Fuchs

Since 2006, when Michael Fuchs opened a New York branch of Haas & Fuchs, the Berlin art gallery he co-owns, the dealer has lived in both cities. Home in Manhattan is a Chelsea penthouse with a wraparound terrace and million-dollar views. Fuchs did no decorating beyond moving in some of the modernist furniture he has acquired over time – Verner Panton, Hans Wegner, and Alvar Aalto are favorites – and installing works from his first-rate art collection. "Nero's Pizza Oven," a 2007 brick and aluminum duct construction by Eric Wesley, sits on the terrace, while Manfred Pernice's 2003 stone and wood "Roswitha" stands next to the fireplace. Mixed in with the bedroom's postwar paintings are four recently acquired works by Giambattista Tiepolo. "I've become interested in old master drawings – contemporary art is just too expensive," Fuchs says with a laugh.

Michael Fuchs, Mitbesitzer der Berliner Galerie Haas & Fuchs, eröffnete 2006 in New York eine Niederlassung. Seither lebt er in beiden Städten. In Manhattan bewohnt er ein Penthouse in Chelsea mit einer rund um die Wohnung führenden Terrasse und spektakulärer Aussicht. Viel Aufwand hat Fuchs für die Einrichtung nicht betrieben und einfach ein paar Lieblingsobjekte aus seinen Sammlungen hineingestellt. Dazu gehören Möbelstücke von Verner Panton, Hans Wegner, Alvar Aalto und hochkarätige Kunstwerke wie „Nero's Pizza Oven", ein Objekt von 2007 aus Aluminiumrohr und Backsteinen von Eric Wesley, das auf der Terrasse steht, und „Roswitha", eine Holz- und Steinskulptur von Manfred Pernice von 2003, neben dem Wohnzimmerkamin. Im Schlafzimmer hat Fuchs zu seinen gesammelten Bildern aus der Nachkriegszeit vier Werke von Giambattista Tiepolo gehängt: „Heute interessieren mich mehr Zeichnungen alter Meister – zeitgenössische Kunst ist einfach zu teuer geworden", lacht Fuchs.

Previous pages: A work by Eric Wesley, sits on the terrace. Swiss artist Sylvie Fleury's carbon-fiber "Mushrooms." In the living room, Hans Wegner armchairs and sideboard sit on Verner Panton rugs.
Above: "Girl on a Swing," a monoprint by Cecily Brown, hangs at the head of the bed.
Right: A small bronze by Leiko Ikemura sits in the bathroom window.
Facing page: The Manhattan skyline with the Empire State Building.

Pages précédentes : Sur la terrasse une œuvre du jeune artiste Eric Wesley. « Mushrooms », de la Suissesse Sylvie Fleury, une sculpture en fibre de carbone. Dans le séjour, des fauteuils et un buffet d'Hans Wegner sont posés sur des tapis de Verner Panton.
En haut : « Girl on a Swing », un monotype de Cecily Brown, est accroché au-dessus du lit.
À droite : Sur le rebord de la fenêtre de la salle de bain, un petit bronze de Leiko Ikemura.
Page de droite : La terrasse panoramique avec l'Empire State Building.

Vorhergehende Seiten: Auf der Terrasse ein Werk des jungen Künstlers Eric Wesley. Schwarze Pilze der Künstlerin Sylvie Fleury mit oszillierender Autolackoberfläche. Im Wohnzimmer auf Teppichen von Verner Panton: Sessel und Sideboard von Hans Wegner. Darüber ein Panton-Leuchter.
Oben: „Girl on a Swing", ein Monoprint von Cecily Brown über dem Bett.
Rechts: Im Badezimmerfenster steht eine kleine Bronzefigur von Leiko Ikemura.
Gegenüberliegende Seite: Die Skyline mit dem Empire State Building.

« J'adore le Glamour Bar de Shanghai », déclare la publicitaire Cindy Gallop. « Le design et l'éclairage y sont superbes. Un jour que je m'y trouvais, je me suis dit que j'aimerais vivre dans un endroit pareil. » C'est désormais chose faite. Le décorateur Stefan Boublil, de l'Apartment Creative Agency, a transformé son nouveau loft en écrin noir. Inondé de lumière le jour, l'appartement spacieux se transforme, la nuit, en un espace théâtral et luxueux où règne une ambiance feutrée de club privé. Boublil a également trouvé d'ingénieuses solutions pour loger la vaste collection d'art de la maîtresse de maison, dont une tronçonneuse Gucci plaquée or du britannique Peter Gronquist, et ses quelques 250 paires de souliers à talon aiguille de créateur. Le loft de 325 mètres carrés était autrefois un locale des YMCA. « Je vis dans l'ancien vestiaire des hommes. Si ça, ce n'est pas du bon feng shui ! ».

Cindy Gallop

"The Glamour Bar in Shanghai is one of my favorites," says advertising executive Cindy Gallop. "It's marvelously designed and lit. Sitting there once I thought: I wish I lived in a place like this." Well, now she does. Designer Stefan Boublil of the Apartment Creative Agency has conjured an all-black interior for Gallop's new loft, and after sundown, what is by day a large, airy, and light-filled home, metamorphoses into a darkly dramatic space with a glossy, private-club vibe. Along with Gallop's fantasies, Boublil had to accommodate her extensive art collection, including a gold-plated Gucci chain saw by the British artist Peter Gronquist, as well as her 250-plus pairs of high-fashion stilettos. The 3,500-square-foot loft is in a former YMCA. "I live in what was the men's locker room," Gallop says. "Awfully good feng shui, don't you think?"

„Die Glamour Bar in Shanghai ist eine meiner Lieblingsbars", sagt Werbemanagerin Cindy Gallop. „Sie ist toll eingerichtet und beleuchtet. Bei einem Besuch dachte ich, wie schön es doch wäre, an einem solchen Ort zu leben." Designer Stefan Boublil von The Apartment Creative Agency hat ihren Wunsch erfüllt und ein ganz in Schwarz gehaltenes Loft gestaltet. Das tagsüber luftige, lichtdurchflutete 325 Quadratmeter große Loft verwandelt sich nachts in einen wirkungsvollen, dunklen Raum mit glamouröser Privatklub-Atmosphäre. Boublils zweite Herausforderung war, Platz zu finden für Gallops umfangreiche Kunstsammlung – darunter die vergoldete Gucci-Kettensäge des britischen Künstlers Peter Gronquist – und die über 250 Designerstilettos der Hausherrin. Gallops Loft war früher eine YMCA-Herberge: „Ich lebe in der ehemaligen Männergarderobe. Das bedeutet sehr gutes Feng-Shui."

Previous pages: During parties, the bathtub, which fills from the ceiling, is turned on to become a dramatic water feature.
Above: Tom Dixon mirror-ball lights hang over the custom-made black glass-and-steel dining table. The ebony and faux-ostrich-skin chairs were inspired by ones used at Dior haute couture shows.
Right: The loft is entirely open, but privacy for the bedroom and other spaces can be created with an apartment-wide system of curtains.

Pages précédentes : La baignoire se remplit depuis le plafond. Quand Gallop reçoit, l'eau est ouverte pour créer un effet de cascade.
En haut : Les boules miroitantes de Tom Dixon sont suspendues au-dessus d'une table en verre noir et acier réalisée sur mesure. Les chaises en ébène et imitation de cuir d'autruche ont été inspirées par celles utilisées pour les défilés de haute couture de Dior.
À droite : Le loft est ouvert mais la chambre et d'autres espaces peuvent être isolés grâce à un système de rideaux courant dans tout l'appartement.

Vorhergehende Seiten: Bei Partys sorgt die Badewanne für ein aufsehenerregendes Wasserspektakel: Das Wasser fließt dabei von der Decke in die Wanne.
Oben: Einzelanfertigung: der Esstisch aus schwarzem Glas und Stahl. Darüber hängen verspiegelte Kugelleuchten von Tom Dixon. Die Stühle aus Ebenholz sind mit einem Straußenleder-Imitat bezogen – als Vorlage dienten Stühle einer Haute-Couture-Show von Dior.
Rechts: Das Loft ist ein einziger offener Raum. Für Privatsphäre sorgt ein Vorhangsystem, das sich durchs ganze Apartment zieht.

New New York Interiors   Cindy Gallop

Right: Gallop's collection of 250-plus pairs of designer shoes is displayed in a lit cabinet that runs the entire length of the loft's street wall. The paintings are by British artist David Piddock, a Gallop favorite.
Below: Gallop already owned much of the furniture, but pieces like the two 19th-century chaises in the living area, fit their new, high-glamour environment perfectly. The two large paintings on the left are by Paul Richards.

À droite : Un meuble illuminé courant tout le long du mur donnant côté rue accueille les quelques deux cent cinquante paires de souliers de créateur de Gallop. Les tableaux sont du britannique David Piddock, un chouchou de la maîtresse de maison.
En bas : Gallop possédait déjà la plupart des meubles mais des pièces telles que les deux lits de repos du 19ᵉ siècle dans le coin salon semblaient avoir été conçues pour son nouvel environnement glamour. Les deux grands tableaux sur la gauche sont de Paul Richard.

Rechts: Gallops umfangreiche Designerschuh-Kollektion wird in einer beleuchteten Vitrine, die sich über die ganze Länge der Loft-Außenwand zieht, ausgestellt. Die Bilder sind von einem ihrer Lieblingskünstler, dem Briten David Piddock.
Unten: Kaum Neues: Gallop brachte fast das gesamte Mobiliar in das Loft mit. Die beiden Liegen aus dem 19. Jahrhundert im Wohnbereich passen perfekt in die superglamouröse Umgebung. Die beiden großen Gemälde auf der linken Seite sind von Paul Richard.

Ce loft de 450 mètres carrés qui appartient à un écrivain et son mari vidéaste, est perché au sommet d'une usine du quartier de la confection. Ce dernier conserve son caractère populaire : « Nous avons encore trois bouchers et deux poissonniers dans le coin », s'émerveille le mari. L'espace était autrefois un atelier d'artiste « récupéré et habité » par des étudiants dans les années 1970. Le couple a demandé au cabinet d'architecture Resolution: 4 Architecture de le réaménager tout en préservant son côté industriel. Les sols en béton et les fenêtres en acier ont été remis en état ; la cuisine, les salles de bain et les espaces de rangement ont été rassemblés dans un bloc central. Les trois chambres sont séparées par des portes coulissantes. Quand toutes ces cloisons sont ouvertes, les enfants peuvent faire la course en tricycle tout autour de l'appartement.

A Garment District Loft

This 4,860-square-foot loft, belonging to a writer and her video editor husband, sits on top of a working factory in the Garment District. The neighborhood retains its blue-collar character. "We still have three butchers and two fishmongers within three blocks," notes the husband. The loft had been an artist's studio and raw living space "built by students in the 1970s." The couple asked Resolution: 4 Architecture to upgrade the interiors without losing their industrial feel. The concrete floors and steel-framed windows were refurbished, while kitchen, baths, and storage were gathered into a central box that left half the apartment open. A growing family is accommodated in three bedrooms, separated by big sliding doors.

Das 450 Quadratmeter große Loft auf dem Dach einer ehemaligen Fabrik im Garment District gehört einer Schriftstellerin und ihrem Mann, einem Video-Cutter. In diesem Bezirk herrscht noch Arbeiterviertelatmosphäre: „Wir haben in Fußnähe noch drei Metzger und zwei Fischhändler", bemerkt der Ehemann. Das Loft wurde in den 1970ern von Studenten gebaut und war ursprünglich ein Künstleratelier, so war der Wohnbereich in einem sehr rohen Zustand. Das neue Besitzerpaar beauftragte Resolution: 4 Architecture, das Loft aufzuwerten, ohne seine industrielle Herkunft preiszugeben: Betonböden und stahlgerahmte Fenster wurden renoviert, Küche, Badezimmer und Stauraum zu einer zentralen Box zusammengefasst. Dadurch bleibt viel offener Raum, etwa die Hälfte der Wohnung, erhalten. Ideal für rasante Dreiradfahrten der Kids! Und hinter großen Schiebetüren sind die drei Schlafzimmer der Familie untergebracht.

Previous pages: *In the kitchen area, a Eero Saarinen chair and oiled walnut table sit under a 1960s Italian pendant light. The original concrete floor was refurbished.*
Above: *Droog Design's amusing chest of drawers is an assemblage of boxes held together by a canvas strap.*
Right: *Vintage Oriental rugs are arranged in overlapping layers.*

Pages précédentes : *Dans le coin cuisine, une chaise d'Eero Saarinen et une table en noyer huilé sous un plafonnier italien des années 1960. Le sol original en béton a été remis en état.*
En haut : *Cette amusante commode de Droog Design est un assemblage de boîtes retenues par une sangle en toile.*
À droite : *Une superposition de vieux tapis d'Orient.*

Vorhergehende Seiten: *Ein Eero-Saarinen-Stuhl und eine geölte Walnussholz-Tischplatte unter der italienischen Hängelampe aus den 1960ern. Der originale Betonboden wurde nur poliert.*
Oben: *Die Kommode von Droog Design besteht aus einer Assemblage schief stehender Schubladen, die von einem Leinengurt zusammengehalten werden.*
Rechts: *Mehrere alte Orientteppiche liegen einfach übereinander.*

Right: The kitchen, baths, and storage are gathered in a central service block that leaves more than half the loft open space.
Below: The husband sewed together thrift-shop cashmere sweaters to make a witty patchwork coverlet for the master bedroom.
Following pages: The service block and the white lacquered kitchen island create a large sculptural form at the middle of the loft.

À droite : La cuisine, les salles de bain et les espaces de rangement sont rassemblés dans un grand bloc central, laissant plus de la moitié du loft ouvert.
En bas : Dans la chambre principale, le mari a cousu de vieux pulls en cachemire trouvés dans des fripes pour créer un dessus-de-lit original.
Pages suivantes : Le bloc central et l'îlot de cuisine laqué blanc créent une grande forme sculpturale au milieu du loft.

Rechts: Küche, Badezimmer und Stauraum sind zu einem zentralen Block zusammengefasst – mehr als die Hälfte des Apartments bleibt so ein offener Raum.
Unten: Der Hausherr nähte aus alten Kaschmirpullovern von Secondhandläden einen witzigen Patchwork-Überwurf fürs Elternbett.
Folgende Seiten: Wie eine Skulptur mitten in dem Loft: die weiß lackierte Kücheninsel als zentraler Block.

« Avant de visiter un lieu, je demande toujours comment est la lumière », déclare Joel Grey. L'acteur ayant travaillé avec des maîtres éclairagistes tels que Geoffrey Unsworth, le chef opérateur de « Cabaret », et étant un photographe accompli lui-même (il a déjà publié deux livres de photographie), il n'y a rien d'étonnant à ce que son loft dans le West Village soit une étude dans l'art de l'éclairage naturel et artificiel. S'il l'a aménagé en grande partie lui-même, il a souvent collaboré avec de grands décorateurs par le passé, dont Albert Hadley. « Je possédais déjà la plupart des œuvres d'art et des meubles », explique-t-il. Ainsi, le grand miroir en bois doré de la salle à manger fut déniché par Hadley pour son premier appartement. Cependant, pour plaire à Grey, une provenance prestigieuse n'est pas une priorité : les fauteuils « Butterfly » de Jorge Ferrari Hardy se trouvaient sur la terrasse d'une de ses anciennes demeures et l'armoire Tramp Art du bureau a été trouvée à San Antonio, Texas.

Joel Grey

"My first question about a space is, how's the light?" says Joel Grey. Given that the actor has worked with such lighting wizards as Geoffrey Unsworth, the cameraman on "Cabaret," and that he's published two books of his own accomplished photographs, it's not so surprising that Grey's West Village loft is a study in the art of natural and artificial illumination. But Grey also brought a lifetime's experience of collaborating with major interior designers – including Albert Hadley, to drop one legendary name – to the task of decorating the raw space, which he did largely unaided. "Most of the furniture and art are from previous homes," Grey says. Hadley found the dining area's large gilt-frame mirror for the actor's first place. Not that Grey insists on grand provenance: The "Butterfly" chairs by Jorge Ferrari Hardy sat on the terrace of a former apartment, and the armoire in the study is a folk-art piece found in San Antonio, Texas.

„Das Wichtigste bei Räumen ist für mich das Licht", sagt Schauspieler Joel Grey. Er hat bereits mit Lichtkünstlern wie Geoffrey Unsworth, dem Kameramann von „Cabaret", zusammengearbeitet und zwei Fotobücher herausgegeben. Sein Loft im West Village ist ebenso eine raffinierte Inszenierung natürlichen und künstlichen Lichts. Grey konnte für die Einrichtung des Rohbaus die jahrelangen Erfahrungen, die er während der Zusammenarbeit mit bekannten Innenarchitekten wie Albert Hadley gesammelt hat, einbringen und brauchte deshalb kaum Hilfe. „Die meisten Möbel und Kunstwerke brachte ich aus meinen früheren Wohnungen mit", sagt Grey. So fand Hadley für seine erste Wohnung den vergoldeten Spiegel im Essbereich. Die Herkunft des Mobiliars ist Grey nicht so wichtig: Die „Butterfly"-Stühle von Jorge Ferrari Hardy standen in seiner früheren Wohnung auf der Terrasse, und der Folk-Art-Schrank im Studierzimmer ist aus San Antonio, Texas.

Previous pages: The loft overlooks the Hudson River. A Richard Tuttle shaped-canvas hangs near the Joe D'Urso-designed dining table. In the study, a school desk faces iconic Al Hirschfeld caricatures of Grey; a folk-art wardrobe occupies the other side of the room.
Facing page: Grey's photograph is of the Prague railway station.
Above: The bedroom area is raised on a wood platform – all other floors are concrete – so that Grey can view the river from his bed.
Right: Grey asked for a large tub set in cast concrete tub after seeing a similar one in a magazine.

Pages précédentes : Le loft domine le fleuve Hudson. Une toile découpée de Richard Tuttle est accrochée près d'une table de Joe D'Urso. Dans le bureau, un pupitre d'écolier fait face à des caricatures de Grey par Al Hirschfeld ; une penderie Folk Art occupe l'autre bout de la pièce.
Page de gauche : Une photographie de la gare de Prague de Grey.
En haut : Alors qu'ailleurs le sol est en béton, la chambre est surélevée sur une plateforme en bois afin que Grey puisse voir le fleuve depuis son lit.
À droite : Grey a commandé une grande baignoire en béton moulé après en avoir vue une similaire dans un magazine.

Vorhergehende Seiten: Vom Loft sieht man auf den Hudson River. Eine interessant geformte Leinwand von Richard Tuttle hinter einem Esstisch von Joe D'Urso. Im Studierzimmer hängen Karikaturen des Kult-Karikaturisten Al Hirschfeld; auf der anderen Seite des Zimmers eine Folk-Art-Garderobe.
Gegenüberliegende Seite: Fotografie des Prager Bahnhofs von Grey.
Oben: Der Schlafbereich ist erhöht, so sieht Grey von seinem Bett auf den Hudson River. Alle anderen Böden sind aus Beton.
Rechts: Grey wünschte sich eine große betongegossene Wanne, wie er sie in einem Magazin gesehen hatte.

Photographe globe-trotter, François Halard, qui possède également une maison du 18ᵉ siècle à Arles, avoue : « Quand je suis à New York, le sud de la France me manque. » Cela explique que son dernier appartement à Manhattan fleure si bon la Provence. Avec son neveu architecte, Bastien Halard, ils ont regroupé un dédale de petits bureaux bas de plafond pour créer une enfilade de pièces spacieuses et claires. À défaut de belles vues, il a accroché ses immenses photographies de la Casa Malaparte, une villa moderniste construite pour l'écrivain Curzio Malaparte sur les rochers de Capri. « Ce sont comme des fenêtres sur le ciel bleu et la mer. » Des copies des canapés de la dite villa, des carreaux provençaux, des rideaux anciens en velours, des tapis marocains et une baignoire en cuivre du 18ᵉ siècle parachèvent l'illusion enchanteresse d'un calme méditerranéen en plein cœur du tumulte new-yorkais.

François Halard

"When I'm in New York, I really miss the south of France," says globetrotting photographer François Halard, whose other residence is an 18th-century house in Arles. So his latest Manhattan apartment, a spacious loft carved from a maze of small, low-ceilinged offices, evokes the Mediterranean. Halard, working with his architect nephew Bastien Halard, created a European-style enfilade of large, airy rooms. The apartment has no views, so Halard conjured some by hanging his enormous photographs of the Casa Malaparte, a modernist house for the writer Curzio Malaparte on a rocky outcrop in Capri. "The pictures are like windows looking out at the blue sky and sea," he says. Copies of sofas from the Villa join Provencal tiles, velvety antique French curtains, Moroccan rugs, and an 18th-century copper bathtub to further the enchanting illusion of Mediterranean calm amidst New York bustle.

„In New York vermisse ich den Süden Frankreichs", sagt der Fotograf François Halard, der auf der ganzen Welt herumreist und in Arles ein Haus aus dem 18. Jahrhundert besitzt. Es erstaunt daher nicht, dass sein Apartment in Manhattan Mittelmeer-Ambiente ausstrahlt. Aus einem Labyrinth kleiner, niedriger Büroräume machte Halard zusammen mit seinem Architekten und Neffen Bastien Halard ein geräumiges Loft – eine Aneinanderreihung großer, luftiger Räume in europäischer Tradition. Die fehlende Aussicht kompensiert er mit riesigen Fotos der Casa Malaparte, dem Modernisten-Haus des Schriftstellers Curzio Malaparte, das auf einem Felsvorsprung der Insel Capri steht. Halard: „Mit Blick auf den blauen Himmel und Meer wirken sie wie Fenster." Auch Halards Einrichtung lässt die Hektik New Yorks vergessen, und man wähnt sich an ruhigen Mittelmeergefilden: Malaparte-Sofa-Kopien, provenzalische Kacheln, antike französische Samtvorhänge, marokkanische Teppiche und eine Kupferbadewanne aus dem 18. Jahrhundert.

Previous pages: French 1950s wood-and-iron bookcases line the library walls, while the 19th-century stage-décor chandelier above the Ico Parisi teak desk is a copy of one in Halard's house in Arles.
Above: Halard designed the living room's green velvet sofa; the rocking chairs are French 1930s, the cowhide rug is from Argentina.
Right: A 19th-century neoclassical Irish mirror sits on a Halard-designed fireplace inspired by Brancusi's atelier in Paris.

Pages précédentes : Dans la bibliothèque, des étagères en bois et fer des années 1950 tapissent les murs. Au-dessus du bureau en teck d'Ico Parisi, le lustre du 19ᵉ siècle, ancien décor de théâtre, est une copie de celui qui orne la maison de Halard à Arles.
En haut : Halard a dessiné le canapé en velours vert du séjour. Les deux rocking-chairs des années 1930 sont français. La peau de vache vient d'Argentine.
À droite : Un miroir néoclassique irlandais du 19ᵉ siècle repose sur la cheminée dessinée par Halard. Elle s'inspire de celle de l'atelier de Brancusi à Paris.

Vorhergehende Seiten: In der Bibliothek: französische Bücherregale aus Holz und Eisen aus den 1950ern. Der Leuchter über dem Teakholz-Tisch von Ico Parisi ist die Kopie eines Leuchters in Halards Haus in Arles.
Oben: Halard entwarf das grüne Samtsofa im Wohnzimmer; die 1930er-Schaukelstühle sind aus Frankreich, das Kuhfell stammt aus Argentinien.
Rechts: Der riesige klassizistische Spiegel aus dem 19. Jahrhundert auf dem Kamin stammt aus Irland. Halard hat den Kamin – inspiriert vom rekonstruierten Atelier Brancusis in Paris – selbst entworfen.

Right: Copies of slipcovered sofas designed for Casa Malaparte sit under Halard's monumental photographs of their original home. Halard covered one of them in blue – just as Jean-Luc Godard did when he filmed "Contempt" at the Casa in the 1960s.
Below: The black-and-white Moroccan rug, bought in Tangier, covers the living room's ebony-stained plywood floor.

À droite : Sous les photographies monumentales de la Casa Malaparte, prises par Halard, des copies des canapés qui se trouvent dans la célèbre villa. Halard en a recouvert un d'une housse bleue, comme Jean-Luc Godard lorsqu'il a filmé « Le Mépris » dans la villa dans les années 1960.
En bas : Sur le plancher du séjour, en contreplaqué teint couleur ébène, un tapis marocain noir et blanc acheté à Tanger.

Rechts: Kopien der Sofas, die eigens für die Casa Malaparte entworfen wurden. Darüber hängen Halards monumentale Fotos der Villa, in der die Originale stehen. Eines der Sofas hat Halard mit stahlblauem Stoff beziehen lassen – als Vorbild diente Jean-Luc Godards Film „Die Verachtung", den dieser in den 1960ern in der Casa Malaparte drehte.
Unten: Ein schwarz-weißer marokkanischer Teppich aus Tanger auf dunkel gebeiztem Sperrholzboden.

Facing page: The original timber beams were exposed during the apartment's gut renovation. French 1950s ceramic sconces flank the window-like print of a Casa Malaparte exterior.
Above: The kitchen's stainless-steel cabinets were custom-made by a restaurant supplier. Vintage factory lights, found at a Marseilles flea market, hang above the 1950s French table.
Right: In the L-shaped kitchen, the French 1940s oak table and chairs sit on a 19th-century tile floor from Avignon.

Page de gauche : Les poutres originales ont été mises à nu lors des travaux de rénovation. Des appliques françaises en céramique, datant des années 1950, flanquent une photo géante de l'escalier de la Casa Malaparte.
En haut : Les placards de la cuisine, en acier inoxydable, ont été réalisés sur mesure par un fournisseur de restaurants. Au-dessus d'une table française des années 1950, de vieux plafonniers industriels dénichés sur un marché aux puces de Marseille.
À droite : Dans la cuisine en L, la table en chêne et les chaises des années 1940 sont françaises. Au sol, un carrelage du 19e siècle provenant d'Avignon.

Gegenüberliegende Seite: Bei der umfassenden Renovierung wurden die Original-Holzbalken freigelegt. Französische Keramik-Wandlampen aus den 1950ern flankieren den Fotoprint einer Außenansicht der Casa Malaparte.
Oben: Die Küchenschränke aus Edelstahl wurden speziell angefertigt. Die alten Fabriklampen über dem französischen Tisch aus den 1950ern fand Halard auf einem Flohmarkt in Marseille.
Rechts: In der L-förmigen Küche stehen ein französischer Eichentisch und französische Eichenstühle aus den 1940ern auf Bodenfliesen aus Avignon aus dem 19. Jahrhundert.

Right: African stools flank the living room's faux fireplace, while an African mask, a photograph of Joseph Beuys, and a Henri Matisse portrait sit on the mantelpiece.
Below: Vintage photographs from the 1930s and 1940s seem to float on the bedroom's sky-blue walls. A vintage suzani covers the 19th-century New England four-poster bed.

À droite : Des tabourets africains flanquent la fausse cheminée du séjour sur laquelle sont posés un masque africain, une photographie de Joseph Beuys et un portrait de Henri Matisse.
En bas : Des photographies des années 1930 et 1940 semblent flotter sur les murs azuréens de la chambre. Un suzani ancien couvre le lit du 19e siècle, provenant de Nouvelle-Angleterre.

Rechts: Afrikanische Hocker flankieren den „falschen" Kamin. Auf dem Sims: eine afrikanische Maske, eine Fotografie von Joseph Beuys und ein Porträt von Henri Matisse.
Unten: Auf den himmelblauen Wänden des Schlafzimmers hängen Fotos aus den 1930ern und 1940ern. Ein alter Suzani deckt das Pfostenbett, das aus New England und aus dem 19. Jahrhundert stammt.

Above: Halard owned the 18th-century copper bath for 15 years
before he found the right place to install it – right under a panel of
18th-century Sicilian tiles.
Right: The entry hall has another Halard-designed faux fireplace;
a 19th-century Buddha perches on the mantle, surrounded by
photographs and drawings by Christian Bérard, among others.

En haut : Halard a conservé la baignoire en cuivre du 18ᵉ siècle pendant quinze ans, avant de lui trouver sa juste place : sous un panneau
de carreaux siciliens du 18ᵉ siècle.
À droite : Dans l'entrée, sur une autre fausse cheminée dessinée par
Halard, trône un bouddha du 19ᵉ siècle. Il est entouré de photos et
de dessins de Christian Bérard, entre autres.

Oben: Die Kupferbadewanne aus dem 18. Jahrhundert war bereits
seit 15 Jahren in Halards Besitz, bevor er den richtigen Platz für sie
fand: Nun steht sie unter einem Wandpaneel mit sizilianischen
Fliesen aus dem 18. Jahrhundert.
Rechts: In der Eingangshalle befindet sich ein weiterer von Halard
entworfener „falscher" Kamin; auf dem Sims ein Buddha aus dem
19. Jahrhundert; rundherum Fotografien und Zeichnungen, unter
anderem von Christian Bérard.

Il y a quelques années, alors qu'il travaillait sur un projet lié au recyclage, le couple de photographes Constance Hansen et Russell Peacock a rencontré les deux principaux membres du cabinet d'architecture écologique LOT-EK, à qui il a confié la métamorphose, sur le principe du recyclage, de leur cabanon enduit de goudron, perché sur un toit de Midtown, en un penthouse de 95 mètres carrés. LOT-EK a transformé la structure en un seul espace souple. De vieux châssis de réfrigérateur ont formé des niches, une carcasse de camion a été remontée sur la terrasse pour servir de lieu de méditation. La plupart des meubles sont d'occasion ou de récupération car, comme le dit Hansen, « On n'est pas très matérialiste », une attitude qui explique que le couple ait été séduit par LOT-EK.

Constance Hansen & Russell Peacock

Working on a recycling-themed photo shoot a few years ago, married photographers Constance Hansen and Russell Peacock met the principals of the eco-aware architecture firm LOT-EK. The architects signed up to do a recycling-based renovation of the photographers' tar-covered shack on a Midtown rooftop, transforming it into a 1,000-square-foot penthouse. LOT-EK turned the structure into one, flexible living space. Niches, in the form of old refrigerator chassis, were inserted in the walls, and a truck-container frame was reassembled on top of the shack as a crow's nest where Hansen meditates. The furniture is mostly second-hand or scavenged, because, she says, "We're not big on stuff." Which is the attitude that led the couple to LOT-EK in the first place.

Vor ein paar Jahren traf das Werbefotografen-Ehepaar Constance Hansen und Russell Peacock bei einem Shooting zum Thema Recycling die Chefs des umweltbewussten Architekturbüros LOT-EK. Die Begegnung führte dazu, dass die Architekten die mit Teerpappe überzogene Baracke des Fotografenpaares auf dem Dach eines Gebäudes in Midtown in ein 95 Quadratmeter großes Penthouse verwandelten. Selbstverständlich unter Anwendung des Recycling-Prinzips. Aber LOT-EK gestaltete aus dem bestehenden Grundriss einen flexiblen Wohnraum. In die Wände wurden alte Kühlschrankgehäuse eingebaut und auf das Dach ein Lastwagencontainer gesetzt, der heute Hansen als Meditationsraum dient. Die Möbel sind fast ausnahmslos aus zweiter Hand oder Stücke, die aus dem Müll gerettet wurden. Hansen: „An Materiellem liegt uns einfach nicht besonders viel." Das war auch der Grund, warum das Paar mit LOT-EK zusammenarbeitete.

Previous pages: LOT-EK used a truck-container frame as a bedroom addition on top of the penthouse.
Facing page: The small window above the desk was made from a metal newspaper street-distribution box.
Above: Niches for electronic components were made by inserting old refrigerator bodies in the walls.
Right: Constance Hansen meditates in the addition upstairs.
Following pages: The shack is now one open living space.

Pages précédentes : LOT-EK a utilisé une carcasse de camion pour créer une extension de la chambre sur le toit.
Page de gauche : La petite fenêtre au-dessus du bureau a été créée avec un distributeur de journaux en métal comme on en trouve dans les rues.
En haut : Les appareils électroniques sont placés dans des niches réalisées avec de vieilles carcasses de réfrigérateur encastrées dans le mur.
À droite : Constance Hansen médite dans l'extension à l'étage.
Pages suivantes : Le cabanon a été transformé en un grand espace ouvert.

Vorhergehende Seiten: In einem auf das Dach gesetzten, alten Lastwagencontainer bauten die LOT-EK-Architekten ein Schlafzimmer.
Gegenüberliegende Seite: Ein alter amerikanischer Zeitungskasten wurde zum kleinen Fenster über dem Schreibtisch.
Oben: Die Unterhaltungselektronik ist in alten, in die Wände integrierten Kühlschrankgehäusen verstaut.
Rechts: Im Schlafraum aus einem alten Lastwagencontainer meditiert Constance Hansen.
Folgende Seiten: Die ehemalige Baracke ist heute ein offener Wohnraum.

La courtière immobilière Jan Hashey a l'habitude des affaires en or mais, en voyant partir comme des petits pains une série de six lofts logés dans d'anciennes écuries de 1909 dans le West Village, elle a compris qu'il lui en fallait un avant qu'il ne soit trop tard. Elle a acheté 280 mètres carrés d'espace vide, puis a demandé à l'architecte Deborah Berke d'en faire l'appartement de trois chambres et deux salles de bain qu'elle partage à présent avec son mari, Yasuo Minagawa. « Deborah a écouté nos besoins et les a traduits en un plan serein et délicat », déclare-t-elle. Berke a conservé les éléments robustes de la structure tels que les fenêtres industrielles mais a recouvert les sols en béton d'un plancher en pin. Plus de dix ans plus tard, Hashey affirme : « Je n'ai jamais vu un appartement contre lequel je serais prête à échanger celui-ci. »

Jan Hashey &
Yasuo Minagawa

Manhattan real estate broker Jan Hashey sees many great apartments. But when she was marketing six lofts in a 1909 former stables and got depressed at each sale, Hashey realized she had to have one of the condominiums herself. So she bought 3,000 square feet of raw space in the West Village building, and hired architect Deborah Berke to turn it into the home Hashey now shares with her husband, Yasuo Minagawa. "Deborah listened to our needs and wrapped a serene and delicate plan around them," says Hashey of the three-bedroom, two-bath layout. Muscular elements like the building's industrial windows remain, though Berke covered the concrete floors with pine planking. More than a decade later, Hashey says, "I've never seen any apartment I'd trade it for."

Jan Hashey ist eine sehr erfolgreiche Immobilienmaklerin in Manhattan und sieht in ihrem Job so manches tolle Apartment. Als sie die sechs Lofts in den ehemaligen Stallungen von 1909 auf den Markt brachte, war sie nach jedem Verkauf nicht etwa glücklich, sondern traurig. Schnell wurde klar: Sie musste eines dieser Lofts im West Village für sich und ihren Ehemann Yasuo Minagawa kaufen. Für den Ausbau der 280 Quadratmeter großen Rohbaufläche engagierte sie die Architektin Deborah Berke, eine Meisterin der elegant-strengen Moderne. Hashey über die Gestaltung der Räumlichkeiten mit drei Schlaf- und zwei Badezimmern: „Deborah hörte sich unsere Bedürfnisse an und setzte sie in einen ruhigen, klaren Grundriss um." An typischen Elementen wie den Industriefenstern änderte Berke wenig. Der Betonboden allerdings wurde mit dunkel gebeizten Kieferndielen belegt. Auch nach zehn Jahren möchte Hashey die Räume mit keinem anderen Apartment tauschen.

Previous pages: *Architect Deborah Berke designed the living room's simple concrete fireplace and adjoining firewood storage cabinet. The floors are 23-inch-wide pine planks, darkened with pigment and mineral oil.*
Right: *In Jan Hashey's home office, the shelves and desk unit are designed by Dieter Rams for Vitsœ.*
Below: *The loft's curtainless, industrial-style windows are close replicas of the century-old building's original fenestration.*

Pages précédentes : *Deborah Berke a dessiné la sobre cheminée en béton ainsi que le meuble adjacent où garder les bûches. Le parquet est en lattes de pin de 58 centimètres de large, noircies avec du pigment et de l'huile minérale.*
À droite : *Dans le bureau de Jan Hashey, les étagères et le bureau ont été dessinés par Dieter Rams pour Vitsœ.*
En bas : *Les fenêtres industrielles, sans rideaux, sont de proches répliques du fenêtrage original du bâtiment, vieux d'un siècle.*

Vorhergehende Seiten: *Architektin Deborah Berke entwarf den einfachen Kamin aus Beton und den dazugehörigen Schrank zur Aufbewahrung des Feuerholzes im Wohnzimmer. Der Boden besteht aus fast 60 Zentimeter breiten Kieferndielen, die mit Pigmenten und Mineralöl dunkel gefärbt wurden.*
Rechts: *In Jan Hasheys Büro Regale und Schreibtisch von Dieter Rams für Vitsœ.*
Unten: *Die vorhanglosen Industriefenster sind Repliken der Originalfenster des 100 Jahre alten Gebäudes.*

Above: In the dining area, laser-cut chairs by Ineke Hans surround
a table custom-made for them by George Smith. The photograph is
by Jessica Craig-Martin, Hashey's daughter.
Right: Although Minagawa is a master frame maker, all the wash
paintings in the study are his own work.
Following pages: A painting by Minagawa hangs above a wooden
tray and a ceramic vessel, both Japanese. Among Hashey's art collection are an Adam Fuss photograph of her then-baby grandson,
Finbar; an Elizabeth Murray painting above a Peter Schlesinger
vase; and an Elizabeth Peyton monoprint in the bathroom.

En haut : Dans le coin salle à manger, des chaises découpées au laser
par Ineke Hans entourent une table réalisée sur mesure par George
Smith. La photographie est de Jessica Craig-Martin, la fille de Hashey.
À droite : Maître encadreur, Minagawa est l'auteur de toutes les
aquarelles dans l'atelier.
Pages suivantes : Un tableau de Minagawa au-dessus d'une assiette
en bois et d'un pot japonais. La collection d'œuvres d'art de Hashey
inclut un portrait de son petit-fils, Finbar, encore bébé, par Adam
Fuss. Une toile d'Elizabeth Murray au-dessus d'un vase de Peter
Schlesinger. Dans la salle de bain, un monotype d'Elizabeth Peyton.

Oben: Stühle der Designerin Ineke Hans um einen Tisch von George
Smith. Das Foto stammt von Hasheys Tochter Jessica Craig-Martin.
Unten: Minagawa ist nicht nur ein virtuoser Rahmenbauer, auch alle
Aquarelle in seinem Arbeitszimmer stammen von ihm.
Folgende Seiten: Japanisches Holztablett und Keramikgefäss auf
dem Schrank für Feuerholz. Darüber hängt ein Bild Minagawas.
Auf dem Fotoprint von Adam Fuss: Hasheys Enkel Finbar als Baby.
Eine Vase von Peter Schlesinger und darüber ein Bild von Elizabeth
Murray. Der Monoprint im Bad ist von Elizabeth Peyton.

L'artiste et ébéniste Tyler Hays savait ce qu'il voulait en concevant
son loft à Brooklyn : un espace silencieux et isolé, sans fenêtres ni
voisins mais rempli de lumière naturelle et, surtout, avec une baignoire en béton moulé en son centre. L'espace unique de 75 mètres
carrés, situé à l'intérieur d'un entrepôt au haut plafond, est la retraite
urbaine idéale : d'un calme serein, baignant dans un éclat à la Vermeer
tombant du ciel. Hays a d'abord placé la baignoire avant de concevoir l'habitation tout autour : une cuisine simple dans un angle, un
lit contre le mur, un coin repas sous une verrière. En guise d'ameublement, il n'a utilisé que ses créations minimalistes et son art qui s'har-
monise parfaitement avec l'environnement dépouillé.

Tyler Hays

Artist and furniture maker Tyler Hays knew what he wanted when
designing a small loft for himself in Brooklyn: a silent, secluded
space, devoid of the distraction of windows or surrounding neigh-
bors above or below, but still with plenty of natural light, and most
importantly, a cast concrete tub as the centerpiece of the place.
The 800-square-foot, single-space dwelling Hays made in the middle of a high-ceilinged warehouse is the ultimate big-city hideout:
a blissfully quiet, sky-lighted retreat that's bathed in Vermeer-like
radiance. Hays positioned the tub first, then oriented the rest of
his one-room home around it: simple kitchen in one corner, sleeping area against a wall, dining area under a skylight. Furnishing
the place was easy. Hays used nothing but his own minimalist
furniture and art, which, unsurprisingly, fit the pared-down environment perfectly.

Der Künstler und Möbeldesigner Tyler Hays wusste genau, was er
wollte, als er sich an die Einrichtung seines kleinen Lofts in Brooklyn
machte: einen ruhigen, abgeschiedenen Raum, ohne störende Nach-
barn und ohne ablenkende Fenster, aber mit viel natürlichem Licht,
und das Wichtigste: eine aus Beton gegossene Wanne im Mittelpunkt.
Das fensterlose 75 Quadratmeter kleine Loft in einer Lagerhalle mit
hohen Decken wurde so zur ultimativen Großstadtoase. Und wie die
Werke Vermeers strahlt der himmlisch ruhige, lichtdurchflutete Rück-
zugsort eine magische Stille aus. Zunächst ließ Hays die große Betonwanne gießen, dann ordnete er alles andere darum an: eine einfache Küche in der Ecke, einen Schlafbereich gegen die Wand, eine
Essecke unter dem Oberlicht. Die Einrichtung ist schlicht: Sie besteht
aus nichts anderem als Hays' eigenen minimalistischen Möbeln und
Kunstwerken. So ist es keine Überraschung, dass alles ganz wunder-
bar zusammenpasst.

Left: The Japanese-inspired tub has no faucets – Hays could find none he liked – so a hand wrench is used to turn the water on. The shower is made of copper, which slowly patinates to green.
Below: The bed is made of unfinished mahogany because Hays liked its "light, peachy tone." The curved bench is of his design, too.

À gauche : La baignoire d'inspiration japonaise n'a pas de robinet, Hays n'en ayant pas trouvé lui convenant. On ouvre l'eau avec une clef à molette. La douche en cuivre se patine lentement de vert-de-gris.
En bas : Le lit en acajou n'a jamais été achevé car Hays aimait son « ton clair, couleur pêche ». Il a également créé la banquette aux bords incurvés.

Links: Die Badewanne im japanischen Stil hat keine Wasserhähne, weil Hays nichts fand, was ihm gefiel. So benutzt er, um Wasser auf-zudrehen, eine Handzange. Im Laufe der Zeit erhielt die Kupfer-dusche eine grüne Patina.
Unten: Hays liebt den hellen, pfirsichfarbenen Ton des unbehandelten Mahagonyholzes seines Bettes. Die Holzbank mit geschwungenen Seiten hat er auch entworfen.

Previous pages: A corner mirror by Hays reflects the skylights in the windowless loft. The concrete bathtub was positioned first, then the loft's other areas were oriented around it. All art and furniture, including the stereo speakers, are of Hays's design and manufacture.
Facing page: Hays finds the rudimentary kitchen unsatisfactory – the only part of the loft he finds inadequate – and intends to install a properly equipped one when he can.

Pages précédentes : Posé dans un coin, le miroir de Hays reflète la verrière de l'espace sans fenêtres. La baignoire en béton a été placée d'abord afin d'aménager le reste du loft tout autour. Les œuvres d'art ainsi que tout le mobilier, y compris les baffles de la chaîne hi-fi, ont été conçus et fabriqués par Hays.
Page de gauche : Hays n'est pas satisfait de sa cuisine rudimentaire et entend en créer une convenablement équipée à la première occasion.

Vorhergehende Seiten: In dem Eckspiegel, ein Entwurf von Hays, spiegelt sich das Oberlicht. Die Betonwanne wurde als Erstes instal-liert, alles andere um diese angeordnet. Ebenfalls von Hays entworfen: Kunstwerke, Möbel und Stereolautsprecher.
Gegenüberliegende Seite: Mit der Küche ist der Hausherr noch nicht ganz zufrieden. Er will sie sobald wie möglich besser ausrüsten.

Riche héritière, égérie de Warhol, collectionneuse et grande mondaine, Jane Holzer a vécu dans des lieux prestigieux mais aucun d'aussi grandiose que sa demeure actuelle, un hôtel particulier néo-renaissance de cinq étages dans le Upper East Side. « Quand je l'ai vu il y a quelques années, j'en suis tombée amoureuse. » Elle s'est contentée de décaper un mur avant d'emménager. Heureusement, elle avait de quoi remplir l'espace considérable : sa collection d'art contemporain – qui inclut naturellement des œuvres de Warhol mais également d'Ed Ruscha, d'Elizabeth Peyton, de Richard Prince – est assez vaste pour remplir un musée. Le meubler ne fut pas un problème non plus. Elle possédait déjà des pièces de Marco Zanuso, de Jacques Adnet, de Karl Springer, de John Dickinson, de Samuel Marx et d'autres sommités du design, qui semblent parfaitement à leur place dans ce décor de palazzo du 16ᵉ siècle.

Jane Holzer

Jane Holzer, heiress, Warhol superstar, art collector, and socialite has lived at some grand addresses, but none grander than her present home, a six-story Renaissance Revival-style townhouse on the Upper East Side. "I saw it a couple of years ago and fell in love with it," says Holzer, who did nothing more than strip some paint from a wall before moving in to the century-old mansion. Fortunately Holzer had enough contemporary art – works by Warhol, of course, but also Ed Ruscha, Elizabeth Peyton, Richard Prince, and such – to fill a large museum, which is about how much wall space she has at her disposal. Furniture wasn't a problem, either. She simply used pieces she already had by Marco Zanuso, Jacques Adnet, Karl Springer, John Dickinson, Samuel Marx, and other modern-design luminaries. Happily, Holzer's 20th-century chattels look right at home in the 16th-century palazzo setting.

Jane Holzer, betuchte Erbin, Warhol-Superstar, Kunstsammlerin und eine New York Socialite hat bereits an einigen grandiosen Adressen gelebt. Doch ihr heutiges Zuhause, ein sechstöckiges Stadthaus im Stil der Renaissance an der Upper East Side übertrifft alles: „Ich verliebte mich sofort, als ich es vor ein paar Jahren entdeckte!" Renovierungen ließ sie kaum vornehmen – einzig die Farbe an den Wänden wurde entfernt. Ein Glück für Holzer, dass ihre zeitgenössische Kunstsammlung umfangreich genug ist, um das riesige Haus, das fast so groß wie ein Museum ist, zu füllen. Darunter befinden sich Werke von Ed Ruscha, Elizabeth Peyton und Richard Prince. Auch ihr Mobiliar – Entwürfe von Marco Zanuso, Jacques Adnet, Karl Springer, John Dickinson, Samuel Marx und anderen bedeutenden modernen Designerikonen – fügte sich perfekt in den Palazzo im Stil des 16. Jahrhunderts ein.

Previous pages: The fireplace in the mansion's foyer is surrounded by Ed Ruscha's "Victory," a Keith Haring sculpture, a Marco Zanuso armchair, and a pair of stools by Raymond Subes.
Right: Three sheep by Claude and François-Xavier Lalanne gather in the dining room. Silver Rudolf Stingel paintings hang above a lacquered chest that once belonged to Consuelo Vanderbilt Balsan.
Below: Warhol's "Liz" and "Round Jackie" hang in the paneled library furnished with armchairs by Jacques Adnet and Marco Zanuso.

Pages précédentes : Au-dessus de la cheminée du hall d'entrée, une toile d'Ed Ruscha, « Victory ». Autour, une sculpture de Keith Haring, un fauteuil de Marco Zanuso et une paire de tabourets de Raymond Subes.
À droite : Trois moutons de Claude et François-Xavier Lalanne montent la garde dans la salle à manger. Au-dessus d'un coffre laqué ayant appartenu à Consuelo Vanderbilt Balsan, deux tableaux en argent de Rudolf Stingel.
En bas : Sur les boiseries de la bibliothèque, deux œuvres de Warhol, « Liz » et « Round Jackie ». Les fauteuils sont de Jacques Adnet et de Marco Zanuso.

Vorhergehende Seiten: Rund um den Kamin im Foyer der Villa: „Victory" von Ed Ruscha, eine Skulptur von Keith Haring, ein Sessel von Marco Zanuso und Hocker von Raymond Subes.
Rechts: Im Esszimmer „weiden" drei Schafe von Claude und François-Xavier Lalanne. Über der lackierten Kommode, die früher Consuelo Vanderbilt Balsan gehörte, hängen silberne Bilder von Rudolf Stingel.
Unten: In der holzvertäfelten Bibliothek: „Liz" und „Round Jackie" von Warhol. Die Sessel sind von Jacques Adnet und Marco Zanuso.

Above: A pair of Christopher Wool paintings loom over the dining room's Karl Springer chairs and table, which has a Richard Prince tire sculpture for a centerpiece.
Right: The sixth-floor living room is awash in Warhol portraits, which Holzer collects.
Following pages: In the library, a Warhol "Jackie" hangs between a mannequin and an Egyptian sarcophagus, both painted black and gold by Keith Haring.

En haut : Dans la salle à manger, deux toiles de Christopher Wool dominent les chaises et la table de Karl Springer. Une sculpture « pneu » de Richard Prince fait office de centre de table.
À droite : Dans le salon du cinquième étage, une collection de portraits par Warhol.
Pages suivantes : Dans la bibliothèque, un « Jackie » de Warhol est accroché entre un mannequin de vitrine et un sarcophage égyptisant, tous deux peints en noir et or par Keith Haring.

Oben: Zwei Bilder von Christopher Wool sowie ein Esszimmertisch und -stühle von Karl Springer. Darauf steht eine Reifenskulptur von Richard Prince.
Rechts: Der Wohnraum im fünften Obergeschoss ist überfüllt mit Warhols aus der Sammlung von Jane Holzer.
Folgende Seiten: In der Bibliothek hängt eine „Jackie" von Warhol zwischen einer Schaufensterpuppe und einem ägyptisierenden Sarkophag – beide von Keith Haring schwarz und gold bemalt.

Le designer et fabricant de meubles Vladimir Kagan et son épouse
Erica Wilson, brodeuse de renom, vivent depuis 1969 dans un im-
mense appartement situé dans un immeuble néogothique des années 1920 sur Park Avenue. Les précédents occupants, propriétaires
du célèbre magasin B. Altman, l'avaient meublé « magnifiquement »
se souvient Kagan. Il y avait une bibliothèque, une vaste réception,
une grande salle à manger. Pour se l'approprier, ils l'ont aménagé
avec des souvenirs de famille importés d'Europe, elle avec son mobilier rapatrié de Londres, lui avec ses antiquités allemandes provenant
de Worms am Rhein, qu'ils ont conjugués avec de l'art et du design
contemporain, la plupart créés par eux-mêmes. Kagan confie : « Nous
avons des maisons à Palm Beach et à Nantucket mais, ici, c'est
notre musée. »

Vladimir Kagan &
Erica Wilson

Since 1969, furniture designer and manufacturer Vladimir Kagan and
his wife, the celebrated needleworker Erica Wilson, have occupied
a rambling Park Avenue apartment in a 1920s neo-Gothic building.
The previous residents, owners of the fabled department store B.
Altman, had furnished the rooms "magnificently, with antiques,"
Kagan recalls. The apartment had a traditional library, vast formal
living room, and large dining room. To put their stamp on the place,
Wilson and Kagan created a décor of European heirlooms – her
British things from London, his German antiques from prewar
Worms am Rhein – blended with contemporary art and pieces
mostly of their own design. "We have homes in Palm Beach and
Nantucket," Kagan says. "But this is our museum."

Der Möbeldesigner und -hersteller Vladimir Kagan lebt seit 1969
zusammen mit seiner Frau, der bekannten Stickerin Erica Wilson,
in einem neugotischen Haus aus den 1920ern an der Park Avenue.
In ihrem weitläufigen Apartment wohnten früher die Besitzer des
legendären Warenhauses B. Altman: „Sie hatten es prachtvoll mit
Antiquitäten eingerichtet", erinnert sich Kagan. Wilson und Kagan
wollten jedoch der Wohnung mit traditioneller Bibliothek, riesigem
Gesellschaftszimmer und großem Esszimmer ihren eigenen Stempel
aufsetzen: Wilson brachte aus London ihre britischen Möbel mit,
Kagan aus Worms am Rhein seine deutschen Vorkriegsantiquitäten.
Dazwischen stellten sie zeitgenössische Kunstwerke und selbst ent-
worfene Objekte. Der Tisch aus den 1950er-Jahren im Wohnzimmer
stammt aus Kagans Junggesellenwohnung, und der Schaukelstuhl
aus Walnussholz ist mit einem Gobelin von Wilson bezogen. „Wir
haben weitere Häuser in Palm Beach und Nantucket", sagt Kagan.
„Dies hier ist aber unser Museum!"

Left: In the dining room, Kagan's saddle-leather and chromed-steel "Fettuccini" chairs pull up to his 1959 "Unicorn" table in teak; Kagan designed the Martini glass for Bombay Sapphire.
Below: The guest bathroom adjoining the library has American mod pattern wallpaper.
Facing pages: Kagan's hourglass chandelier hangs in the carefully restored 1930s kitchen; the Italian chairs are among the few contemporary pieces not of Kagan's design.

À gauche : Dans la salle à manger, les chaises « Fettuccini » de Kagan, en cuir de selle et acier chromé, devant sa table en teck « Unicorn », de 1959. Kagan a dessiné le verre à martini pour Bombay Sapphire.
En bas : Dans la salle de bain des invités, qui jouxte la bibliothèque, un papier peint américain avec un motif Mod.
Page de droite : Dans la cuisine des années 1930, soigneusement restaurée, le lustre « sabliers » de Kagan. Les chaises italiennes comptent parmi les rares meubles contemporains que Kagan n'ait pas dessinés.

Links: Im Esszimmer: Kagans „Fettuccini"-Stühle aus Chromstahl und Sattelleder um den „Unicorn"-Teak-Tisch von 1959; das Martiniglas hat Kagan für Bombay Sapphire entworfen.
Unten: Die Tapeten im Gästebad neben der Bibliothek im amerikanischem Mod-Muster.
Gegenüberliegende Seite: In der sorgfältig renovierten Küche aus den 1930ern: Kagans Sanduhrleuchter und die italienischen Stühle, die zu den wenigen modernen Stücken gehören, die nicht von Kagan entworfen wurden.

Previous pages: The living room includes Kagan's "Omnibus" sofa, "Infinity" steel-and-glass table, and 1952 rocking chair upholstered in Wilson's crewelwork. Wilson's needlepoint throw pillows, and a velvet cushion she made to Kagan's design, sit before a Frank Stella canvas. Clockwise from top left: Windsor chairs surround a 1950s Kagan sculpted table; Kagan's "Tri-Symmetric" lounge chair in red leather; Kagan's 1950s walnut convertible sofa in the library; a Jason Crum painting next to Kagan's 1992 "Corkscrew" chairs.

Pages précédentes : Dans le séjour, le canapé « Omnibus » de Kagan, une table en verre et acier « Infinity » et un rocking-chair de 1952 recouvert d'une tapisserie de Wilson. Devant une toile de Frank Stella, de petits coussins en tapisserie de Wilson et un grand coussin qu'elle a réalisé en patchwork de velours d'après un carton de Kagan. De gauche à droite dans le sens des aiguilles d'une montre : des chaises Windsor autour d'une table sculptée par Kagan dans les années 1950 ; le fauteuil en cuir rouge « Tri-Symmetric » de Kagan ; dans la bibliothèque, un canapé-lit en noyer des années 1950, conçu par Kagan ; une toile de Jason Crum derrière un lampadaire créé par Kagan et ses fauteuils « Corkscrew », de 1992.

Vorhergehende Seiten: Im Wohnzimmer: Kagans „Omnibus"-Systemsofa, ein „Infinity"-Tisch aus Chromstahl und Glas und der Schaukelstuhl von 1952, bezogen mit einer Stickarbeit von Wilson. Vor dem Frank-Stella-Bild Sofakissen mit Stickarbeiten von Wilson und ein Collage-Samtkissen, das Wilson nach einer Vorlage von Kagan nähte. Von oben links im Uhrzeigersinn: Windsor-Stühle um einen Kagan-Tisch aus den 1950ern; ein „Tri-Symmetric"-Kagan-Lounge-Sessel aus rotem Leder; in der Bibliothek ein verstellbares Walnussholzsofa aus den 1950ern und „Corkscrew"-Sessel von 1992.

New New York Interiors   Vladimir Kagan & Erica Wilson

Dans cette maison en grès brun à Brooklyn, construite en 1875, l'art est la vie et vice-versa pour le galeriste Paul Kasmin et son épouse Alexandra. Des trésors y migrent parfois depuis sa galerie à Manhattan qui représente, entre autres, David Hockney, Frank Stella et Kenny Scharf. Par exemple, il a offert à sa femme le mouflon-secrétaire en bronze du petit salon après avoir organisé une exposition des sculpteurs Claude et François-Xavier Lalanne. Alexandra qualifie affectueusement de « grande pagaïe » le décor hétéroclite de leur demeure, qui va du Andy Warhol au-dessus de la cheminée aux silhouettes d'Elliott Puckette de la chambre. Voyageuse invétérée, elle achète plus d'objets aux quatre coins de la planète que sa maison peut en contenir, d'où l'intérêt de son magasin d'arts décoratifs dans le nord de l'état de New York. « Tout ce qui ne rentre pas chez nous va dans la boutique. »

Alexandra & Paul Kasmin

Art is life and vice versa in the 1875 Brooklyn brownstone of New York dealer Paul Kasmin and his wife, Alexandra. Treasures sometimes migrate home from Paul's eponymous Manhattan art gallery, which represents David Hockney, Frank Stella, and Kenny Scharf. For example, Paul's gift to Alexandra, a bronze wild sheep desk in the parlor, came from a show he gave French sculptors Claude and François-Xavier Lalanne. Alexandra calls the home's blend of furnishings – from the Andy Warhol over the mantel to the Elliott Puckette silhouettes in a bedroom – "a big mess, but I like it that way." An inveterate traveler, her global shopping yields more than one house can hold. And that, she says, is where her own decorative arts gallery in upstate New York comes in. "Whatever doesn't go home goes up to the shop."

Das Backsteinhaus in Brooklyn von 1875 gehört dem New Yorker Kunsthändler Paul Kasmin und seiner Frau Alexandra. Das Paar zieht keine klare Grenze zwischen Kunst und Leben. So kommt es vor, dass Paul Kasmin aus seiner gleichnamigen Galerie in Manhattan – er vertritt David Hockney, Frank Stella, Jules Olitski und Kenny Scharf – Kunstwerke mit nach Hause bringt. Etwa als Geschenk für seine Frau, wie den Bronzeschreibtisch von den französischen Bildhauern Claude und François-Xavier Lalanne. Alexandra Kasmin reist ständig umher, um für ihre Kunsthandwerk-Galerie in Upstate New York neue Objekte aufzustöbern. Davon finden auch einige in ihrem Haus in Brookyln ein Zuhause. Sie bezeichnet ihre Einrichtung als „riesige, aber gefällige Unordnung". Und die reicht immerhin vom Andy Warhol über dem Kamin bis zu den Silhouettenbildern von Elliott Puckette rund ums Schlafzimmerfenster.

Previous Pages: Both the bronze desk and Ginkgo chair in the parlour are the work of sculptors Claude and François-Xavier Lalanne.
Facing page: For the master bedroom, Kasmin artist Elliott Puckette painted silhouettes of each of the family's four members.
Above: Hans Wegner chairs surround a new Saarinen table.
Right: Works by Keith Haring and Kenny Scharf hang in the younger daughter's bedroom, with its bunk beds.

Pages précédentes : Dans le petit salon, un secrétaire en bronze et une chaise en ginkgo de Claude et François-Xavier Lalanne.
Page de gauche : Dans la chambre des parents, Elliott Puckette, représenté par Kasmin, a peint les silhouettes des quatre membres de la famille.
En haut : Dans le séjour, des chaises de Hans Wegner autour d'une table d'Eero Saarinen.
À droite : Dans la chambre de la benjamine, avec ses lits superposés, des œuvres de Keith Haring et de Kenny Scharf.

Vorhergehende Seiten: Der Bronzeschreibtisch und der Ginkgo-Stuhl im Salon haben die Bildhauer Claude und François-Xavier Lalanne geschaffen. Sie werden von Paul Kasmins Galerie vertreten.
Gegenüberliegende Seite: Die Künstlerin Elliott Puckette malte von allen vier Kasmin-Familienmitgliedern Silhouetten.
Oben: Hans-Wegner-Stühle rund um einen neuen Saarinen-Tisch.
Rechts: Keith Haring und Kenny Scharf hängen neben einem Etagenbett im Schlafzimmer der jüngeren Kasmin-Tochter.

Le loft de 465 mètres carrés d'Alex Katz, mi-atelier mi-habitation, a l'élégance sobre et nette de ses peintures. À l'instar de ses portraits et paysages, ses quartiers, qui occupent tout un étage, sont inondés de lumière naturelle. Les quelques meubles sont clairement définis dans l'espace, regroupés devant des murs blancs sur un sol acrylique. D'un seul regard, on embrasse tous les détails des pièces principales mais, comme dans l'œuvre mystérieuse et puissante de Katz, sous une apparence simple se cachent de la rigueur et de la maîtrise. Voilà quarante ans qu'il le raffine. Le bloc de cuisine, explique-t-il, « est la simplicité même. Une cuisinière, un lave-vaisselle et un évier encastré dans un plan de travail en formica. Mais j'ai mis sept ou huit ans à le concevoir ». Pourtant, comme sa vie et son art, il semble couler de source.

Alex Katz

Alex Katz's 5,000-square-foot loft – one half studio, the other half home – has the clean, stripped-down stylishness of his paintings. Like his portraits and landscapes, the floor-through quarters are filled with natural light, and the furnishings in them are isolated and clearly defined in space – simple groupings set against white walls and poured-acrylic floors. You can see everything in the main rooms at a glance, as if they were arranged for quick comprehension. But, as with Katz's mysteriously powerful art, there's rigor and mastery under the uncomplicated surface. Katz has been refining the loft for 40 years. "The kitchen unit is the smoothest thing," he says, by way of example. "It's just a stove, dishwasher, and sink enclosed in Formica, but it took seven or eight years to develop." Yet like so much in Katz's life and art, it seems both effortless and inevitable.

Das 465 Quadratmeter große Loft des Künstlers Alex Katz hat die makellose, reduzierte Eleganz seiner Bilder. In der einen Hälfte befindet sich sein Atelier, in der anderen lebt er. Die durchgehenden Räume sind – genau wie Katz' Porträts und Landschaften – durchflutet von natürlichem Licht. Die Möbel darin sind streng voneinander abgegrenzt und stehen in einfachen Arrangements in Kontrast zu den weißen Wänden und gegossenen Acrylböden. Alles wirkt auf den ersten Blick selbstverständlich – doch bei genauerer Betrachtung entdeckt man eine streng durchdachte Komposition und meisterhaftes Können, wie auch in Katz' mystisch-ausdrucksvoller Kunst. Sein Loft perfektioniert er kontinuierlich seit 40 Jahren. Zum Beispiel die Küche: „Herd, Geschirrspüler und Spülbecken sind ganz einfach in einen Formica-Block gegossen. Die Entwicklung daran dauerte aber sieben, acht Jahre." Typisch für sein Leben und für seine Kunst: Es wirkt wie zufällig und mühelos hingestellt.

Previous pages: Half of the loft is a painting studio, half of it the artist's residence. A short hallway connects the two sides.
Right: The studio's steel desk, which has a linoleum top, came from the offices of the "New York Journal-American" newspaper, which ceased publication in 1966.
Below: Two of Katz's paintings from the mid-1990s, "Black Scarf" and "Vivien," lean against the studio wall. The display of cutouts is a complete work, "Green Table (17 heads)," from the same period.

Pages précédentes : Une moitié du loft est un atelier, l'autre une habitation. Un petit couloir sépare les deux.
À droite : Dans l'atelier, le bureau en acier recouvert de linoléum provient des bureaux du « New York Journal American », un quotidien qui a cessé de paraître en 1966.
En bas : Deux toiles peintes par Katz au milieu des années 1990, « Black Scarf » et « Vivien », adossées au mur de l'atelier. Les silhouettes découpées forment une seule et même œuvre, « Green Table (17 heads) », qui date de la même période.

Vorhergehende Seiten: Die eine Hälfte des Lofts ist ein Maleratelier, die andere die Wohnung des Künstlers. Ein kurzer Flur verbindet die beiden Teile.
Rechts: Der Schreibtisch aus Stahl mit Linoleumoberfläche im Atelier stand ursprünglich in den Büros des „New York Journal-American", einer Zeitung, die 1966 eingestellt wurde.
Unten: An der Atelierwand lehnen die beiden Katz-Werke „Black Scarf" und „Vivien" aus den 1990ern. Aus der gleichen Zeit stammt die Anordnung ausgestanzter Silhouetten, die das Werk mit dem Titel „Green Table (17 heads)" bilden.

Above: In the living area, a velvet-covered Victorian couch is paired with a 1960s leather sofa by Robert Haussmann. Katz made the coffee table by placing a slab of marble on the base of a vintage jewelry cabinet. The two paintings are part of Katz's "Man in White Shirt" series from the 1990s.
Right: Katz's studio is as pristine as his paintings.
Following pages: The painting in the dining area, "Swamp Maple," 1968, now hangs in the National Gallery of Art in Washington, DC. Katz designed the free-standing kitchen unit.

En haut : Dans le coin séjour, un divan victorien tapissé de velours côtoie un canapé en cuir des années 1960 de Robert Haussmann. Katz a réalisé la table basse en posant une dalle de marbre sur un ancien présentoir à bijoux. Les deux tableaux font partie de la série « Man in White Shirt » peinte par Katz dans les années 1990.
À droite : L'atelier de Katz est aussi sobre que ses peintures.
Pages suivantes : La toile accrochée dans le coin salle à manger, « Swamp Maple » (1968) se trouve aujourd'hui à la National Gallery of Art de Washington. Katz a conçu lui-même le bloc de cuisine.

Oben: Im Wohnraum steht ein mit Samt bezogenes viktorianisches Sofa neben einer Ledercouch von Robert Haussmann aus den 1960ern. Der Beistelltisch ist eine Eigenkreation. Katz legte dafür eine Marmorplatte auf eine ehemalige Schmuckvitrine. Die zwei Bilder an der Wand sind Teil von Katz' Serie „Man in White Shirt" aus den 1990ern.
Rechts: Das Atelier ist so klar und reduziert wie seine Bilder.
Folgende Doppelseiten: Das Gemälde „Swamp Maple" von 1968 im Essbereich hängt mittlerweile in der National Gallery of Art in Washington D.C. Der frei stehende Küchenblock ist ein Entwurf des Künstlers.

Quand on entre dans l'immeuble de deux étages à Chinatown où Terence Koh vit, travaille et expose ses œuvres, on croit pénétrer dans une de ses installations. À l'exception du club privé au sous-sol, plus sombre qu'une mine de charbon, tous les murs, plafonds, meubles et objets sont blancs. « Je l'appelle mon vaisseau blanc », dit-il. « Je suis un grand fan de la peinture Super White. » (Il cache ses livres et ses objets de couleur dans une « chambre secrète » à l'étage). Un des murs de la cuisine, fonctionnelle car son compagnon aime cuisiner, est tapissé de ces boîtes en Plexiglas que Koh affectionne particulière-ment. L'une d'elle, plus grande, trône au milieu du salon, contenant un paon albinos dont la queue coupée s'étire derrière lui telle une ombre laiteuse. « Les invités s'assoient par terre, à la japonaise », explique Koh. L'expérience esthétique vaut bien cet inconfort mineur.

Terence Koh

Entering the three-story Chinatown building where artist Terence Koh lives, works, and exhibits, is like stepping into one of his art installations. Apart from the private club in the basement, painted black as a coalmine, all the interiors – walls, floors, ceilings, furni-ture, and knickknacks – are entirely white. "I call it my white ship," Koh says. "I'm a big fan of 'Super White' paint." (He hides books and other colored objects in a "secret bedroom" upstairs.) Vitrines, another Koh signature, are piled high against one wall in the kitchen, which is fully functional since Koh's boyfriend likes to cook. The only thing in the living room is a large vitrine containing an albino peacock whose tail has fallen off and extends behind it like a milky shadow. "Guests sit on the floor, Japanese style," Koh says – a small discomfort for an enveloping aesthetic experience.

In diesem dreistöckigen Haus in Chinatown, in dem der Künstler Terence Koh lebt, arbeitet und ausstellt, fühlt man sich wie in einer seiner Installationen. Im Inneren – von den Wänden, Böden, Decken, Möbeln bis zu den Nippes – ist alles weiß. „Mein weißes Schiff", sagt Koh, „ich bin ein großer Fan der Farbe „Super White". Einzig der Privatklub im Keller ist kohlrabenschwarz. Alles Farbige wie Bücher und Objekte verstaut er in einem „geheimen Schlafzimmer" im Obergeschoss. In der vollständig ausgerüsteten Küche – Kohs Partner kocht gerne – stapeln sich an einer Wand typische Koh-Vitri-nen. Das einzige Objekt im Wohnzimmer ist ebenfalls eine Vitrine, in der ein Albino-Pfau seinen abgefallenen Schwanz zur Schau stellt. „Bei uns sitzen die Gäste wie in Japan auf dem Boden", sagt Koh. In Anbetracht des visuellen Gesamterlebnisses ist dies jedoch nur eine kleine, in Kauf zu nehmende Unbequemlichkeit.

Previous pages: Koh uses a wall in the working kitchen to stack the vitrines he often uses in his art installations.
Right: Koh broke off the heads of the Dresden shepherd and shepherdess figurines at the base of a table lamp, then dipped the whole thing in white paint.
Below: The only "furniture" in the living room is a vitrine containing a stuffed albino peacock whose tail has fallen off.

Pages précédentes : Koh empile les vitrines qu'il utilise fréquemment dans ses installations contre un mur de sa cuisine.
À droite : Koh a coupé les têtes du berger et de la bergère en porcelaine de Dresde et les a plongés dans de la peinture blanche pour les transformer en pied de lampe.
En bas : Le seul « meuble » du séjour : une vitrine contenant un paon empaillé ayant perdu sa queue.

Vorhergehende Seiten: Aufeinandergestapelte Vitrinen an der Küchenwand: Sie sind auch typischer Bestandteil seiner Kunstinstallationen.
Rechts: Von den Dresdner Schäfer- und Schäferinfiguren aus Porzellan am Fuße der Tischlampe hat Koh die Köpfe abgebrochen und tauchte das Ganze dann in weiße Farbe.
Unten: Das Wohnzimmer mit dem einzigen „Möbelstück" des Raums, der Vitrine mit einem ausgestopften Albino-Pfau, dessen Schwanz abgefallen ist.

Above: *The second floor acts as a studio for "The Terence Koh Show,"*
a cable television talk program that the artist stages and hosts.
Right: *A private club occupies the basement level of the building, all*
of which, including the toilet, is painted jet black.
Following pages: *The ground-floor gallery is usually left completely*
empty; on this occasion, the floor is covered with packages of prints
about to be shipped out to an exhibition.

En haut : *Le premier étage sert de studio d'enregistrement pour le*
« Terence Koh Show », un talk-show animé par l'artiste pour une
chaîne du câble.
À droite : *Le club privé qui occupe le sous-sol de l'immeuble est*
entièrement peint en noir d'encre, y compris les toilettes.
Pages suivantes : *D'ordinaire, la galerie du rez-de-chaussée est*
laissée totalement vide. Ce jour-là, le sol était jonché de paquets
d'épreuves prêts à être envoyés dans une exposition.

Oben: *Im Obergeschoss liegt das Studio für „The Terence Koh Show",*
eine vom Künstler inszenierte und moderierte Kabelfernseh-Talkshow.
Rechts: *Im Kellergeschoss befindet sich ein Privatklub. Hier wurde*
alles, Toilette inklusive, kohlrabenschwarz gestrichen.
Folgende Seiten: *Die Galerie im Erdgeschoss ist normalerweise leer;*
auf dem Foto hier ist der Boden voller Kartonagen mit Prints, die zu
einer Ausstellung geschickt werden sollen.

Quand, au milieu des années 1970, Joseph Kosuth emménagea dans ce loft qui occupe tout le quatrième étage d'un immeuble à Soho, les rues étaient désertes. Ce n'est plus le cas aujourd'hui. Avec l'arrivée des foules, les loyers ont grimpé en flèche, ce qui a récemment poussé l'artiste à migrer plus au sud de Manhattan. L'espace accueillait autrefois un atelier de confection de chemises (« J'ai trouvé des boutons pendant dix ans », se souvient-il). Kosuth a conservé une bonne partie des détails d'origine – les plafonds métalliques, les murs en plâtre – et unifié les pièces avec une palette noire, grise et blanche. Pendant trente ans, le loft, mi-atelier mi-habitation, a nourri sa créativité ainsi que celle de ses amis. « Pour un de mes anniversaires, David Byrne et John Cale y ont fait une jam. » Ce concert improvisé n'est plus qu'un beau souvenir pour les chanceux qui y ont assisté, tout comme le loft et le quartier d'artistes que Kosuth a contribué à lancer.

Joseph Kosuth

When artist Joseph Kosuth set up his fifth-floor loft – half studio, half residence – in mid-1970s Soho, the weekend streets were empty. Not so today. Along with the crowds have come skyrocketing rents, which recently drove Kosuth to relocate further downtown. The raw, floor-through space in a former shirt factory ("I'd find buttons for ten years," he says) had two street frontages, so Kosuth kept an uninterrupted vista from front to back. He retained much original detail – tin ceilings, plaster walls – while using a unifying palette of black, gray, and white. For three decades, the loft nurtured creativity in the artist – and his friends. "David Byrne and John Cale surprised me one birthday by jamming together," Kosuth recalls. The unrecorded and never repeated concert is now a memory for the lucky attendees, much like the loft and the art-friendly neighborhood Kosuth helped pioneer.

In den 1970ern lebte und arbeitete der Künstler Joseph Kosuth in einem Loft in Soho. Damals waren die Straßen des heute belebten Soho an den Wochenenden völlig leer und die Mieten günstig. Heute sind sie fast unbezahlbar geworden. Grund für Kosuth, weiter Richtung Downtown zu ziehen. Er bezog einen offenen Raum in einer ehemaligen Hemdenfabrik („hier werde ich noch in zehn Jahren alte Knöpfe finden!") mit je einer Straßenfront vorne und hinten und durchgehender Sicht. Viele der Originaldetails wie die Blechdecke und Gipswände ließ er stehen, und er wählte eine einheitliche Farbpalette in Schwarz, Grau und Weiß. Seit drei Jahrzehnten ist das Loft Nährboden für die Kreativität des Künstlers – und auch die seiner Freunde wie die Musiker David Byrne und John Cale. „Die beiden überraschten mich an einem Geburtstag mit einer Jam-Session", erzählt Kosuth. Das Konzert gibt's nicht als Aufnahme, bleibt aber eine schöne Erinnerung für alle, die dabei waren.

Previous pages: Kosuth defined the open dining area by covering the walls, plinth, and lowered ceiling in white tiles, which vary in size to avoid the harsh visual effect of an uninterrupted grid. The 16th-century French dining table is flanked by 19th-century Swedish farm benches; artist Alex Hay designed the television stand originally as a chair.
Right: The limited color palette in the loft – mostly black, gray, and white – is warmed by the use of furniture in natural woods.
Below: Kosuth's "Ex Libris #1-#5," a work in cast metal with paint from 1989, hangs above the sofa.

Pages précédentes : Kosuth a tapissé les murs, les plinthes et le faux-plafond du coin repas de carreaux blancs de tailles différentes afin de définir l'espace tout en évitant l'effet d'uniformité. La table française du 16ᵉ siècle est flanquée de bancs de ferme suédois du 19ᵉ siècle. Le meuble de télévision avait été conçu au départ comme une chaise par l'artiste Alex Hay.
À droite : La palette restreinte du loft – principalement du noir, du gris et du blanc – est réchauffée par le bois naturel des meubles.
En bas : « Ex-Libris #1-#5 », une œuvre de Kosuth de 1989 en métal moulé et peinture, est accrochée au-dessus du canapé.

Vorhergehende Seiten: Im offenen Essbereich versah Kosuth Wände, Sockel und die abgehängte Decke mit verschieden großen weißen Kacheln. Die räumliche Abgrenzung wirkt dadurch fließend. Der französische Esstisch ist aus dem 16. Jahrhundert, die schwedischen Bauernbänke aus dem 19. Jahrhundert; der Fernsehsockel war ursprünglich ein vom Künstler Alex Hay entworfener Stuhl.
Rechts: Die reduzierte Farbpalette im Loft setzt hauptsächlich auf Schwarz, Grau und Weiß.
Unten: Über dem Sofa hängt das Werk Kosuths „Ex Libris #1-#5" von 1989 aus gegossenem Metall und Farbe.

Above: The large, glass-fronted bookcases in Kosuth's studio were salvaged from a soon-to-be demolished villa in upstate New York. The strip of text and white neon running around the top of the walls is a 1986 Kosuth work, "Zero and Not #15," from a series related to Sigmund Freud.
Right: In the studio, another work by Kosuth incorporates images of Freud derived from portraits taken at different points in the psychoanalyst's life.

En haut : Les grandes bibliothèques vitrées de l'atelier de Kosuth furent récupérées dans une villa sur le point d'être démolie dans le nord de l'État de New York. Le texte défilant et le néon blanc en haut des murs est une œuvre de Kosuth de 1986, « Zero and Not #15 », appartenant à une série sur Sigmund Freud.
À droite : Dans l'atelier, une autre œuvre de Kosuth intègre des images de Freud inspirées de portraits réalisés à différentes époques de sa vie.

Oben: Die großen Bücherschränke mit Glasfronten in Kosuths Atelier sind aus einer Villa in Upstate New York, die bald abgerissen werden sollte. Das Kosuth-Werk „Zero and Not #15" (1986) über den Schränken besteht aus weißem Neontext und ist Teil einer Serie, die durch Sigmund Freud inspiriert wurde.
Rechts: Im Atelier ein weiteres Werk Kosuths mit Porträts von Freud, die in verschiedenen Lebensphasen des Psychoanalytikers aufgenommen wurden.

« Le vide, c'est ennuyeux », disait l'architecte Robert Venturi dans les années 1960, se rebiffant contre l'esthétique dépouillée du modernisme pur et dur. Quarante ans plus tard, Cary Leibowitz, directeur des éditions contemporaines chez Phillips de Pury & Company, en a fait sa devise, transformant sa maison de trois étages à Harlem en ode au motif imprimé – sur les murs, les sols, les tissus et les objets. Avec des papiers peints géométriques et floraux des années 1970 comme toile de fond, il a rempli les pièces de meubles et d'art, du plus chic au plus ringard, du plus classique au plus kitsch. Quand il place une sérigraphie de Warhol près de poubelles des années 1960 aux couleurs de la soupe Campbell, ce n'est pas de l'ironie, mais de l'amour. Comme Venturi, il est sensible à l'énergie de la vulgarité pop. Ce qui est aussi bien puisque l'architecte anticonformiste est en train de construire une maison de campagne pour lui et son compagnon, Simon Lince.

Cary Leibowitz

"Less is a bore," architect Robert Venturi said back in the 1960s, challenging the stripped-down aesthetics of orthodox modernism. Forty years later, Cary Leibowitz, mindful of Venturi's dictum, has decorated his four-story Harlem townhouse to the gills. Leibowitz, the director of contemporary editions at Phillips de Pury & Company, is a dedicated follower of pattern – on walls, floors, fabrics, and objects. Using 1970s geometric and floral wallpapers as background, he has filled the rooms with a hoard of furniture and art that runs the gamut from high to low, classic to kitsch. When he puts a Warhol silk-screen next to 1960s Campbell's-soup trash cans, Leibowitz isn't being ironic; he loves them both. Like Venturi, he responds to the energy and life in pop vulgarity, which is a good thing since the maverick architect is designing a country house for Leibowitz and his partner, Simon Lince.

In den 1960ern provozierte der Architekt Robert Venturi mit dem Ausspruch „less is a bore" (weniger ist langweilig) die orthodoxen Vertreter der Moderne und stellte ihre reduzierte Ästhetik infrage. Vierzig Jahre später erlebt Venturis Kampfansage im vierstöckigen Stadthaus von Cary Leibowitz in Harlem ein Revival. Leibowitz, Director of Contemporary Editions bei Phillips de Pury & Company, hat eine besondere Vorliebe für Muster. Er mag sie auf Wänden, Böden, Stoffen und Objekten. In seinem Haus bilden Tapeten mit geometrischen und floralen Mustern aus den 1970ern die Kulisse, vor der er Möbel und Kunstwerke aller Art inszeniert. Kostbar und billig, klassisch und kitschig. Wenn Leibowitz einen echten Warhol-Siebdruck neben billigen „Campbell Soup"-Dosen stellt, so meint er das nicht etwa ironisch, sondern macht beides gleichwertig. Die Vulgarität der Popkultur gefällt ihm – genau wie Venturi, der für Leibowitz und seinen Partner, Simon Lince, gerade ein Landhaus baut.

Left: The living room's vintage wallpaper was found in Germany; Saul's painting "Gun Moll" is flanked by a Wendell Castle "Molar" chair and an Ettore Sottsass "Westside" chair.
Below: Leibowitz stands beside a Warhol portrait of Jimmy Carter.
Following pages: Objects and artworks include liquor display bottles; a genuine Warhol cow next to Warhol-inspired trash cans; reproduction French furniture upholstered in Black Panther power fists; and a Jonathan Borofsky painting over the guest bed. In the dining room, Robert Venturi chairs flank a 1970s Italian table.

À gauche : Le papier peint vintage du séjour a été déniché en Allemagne ; Une toile de Peter Saul, « Gun Moll », est accrochée entre un fauteuil « Molar » de Wendell Castle et un fauteuil « Westside » d'Ettore Sottsass.
En bas : Leibowitz se tient devant un portrait de Jimmy Carter.
Pages suivantes : Parmi les objets et les œuvres d'art, des bouteilles d'alcool géantes ; une authentique vache de Warhol, près de poubelles inspirées de son œuvre ; des copies de canapés français tapissés avec le symbole des Black Panthers ; au-dessus du lit de la chambre d'amis, un tableau de Jonathan Borofsky au rêve. Dans la salle à manger, des chaises de Robert Venturi autour d'une table italienne des années 1970.

Links: Im Wohnzimmer: eine Vintage-Tapete aus Deutschland; das Bild „Gun Moll" von Peter Saul zwischen dem „Molar-Sessel" von Wendell Castle und dem „Westside-Sessel" von Ettore Sottsass.
Unten: Leibowitz vor dem Warhol-Porträt von Jimmy Carter.
Folgende Seiten: Verschiedene Objekte und Kunstwerke: überdimensionierte Ausstellungsflaschen von Spirituosen; das Kuhbild ist ein echter Warhol, die „Campbell"-Dosen sind von Warhol inspiriert; Kopien französischer Sitzmöbel mit einem Stoffmuster aus „Black Panther"-Kampffäusten; über dem Gästebett ein Bild von Jonathan Borofsky, das viele Träume verspricht. Im Esszimmer neben dem italienischen Tisch aus den 1970ern Stühle von Robert Venturi.

Previous pages: The walls of the townhouse staircase are used as an art gallery, with works as diverse as Andy Warhol's portrait of Robert Mapplethorpe and Peter Saul's depiction of a crucified Angela Davis; the 1970s geometric wallpaper is from Belgium.
Facing page: The foyer's walls and ceiling are entirely mirrored, adding to the sense of limitless decorative abundance. In the living room, a John Kacere panties painting looks down on a Frank Stella tapestry rug.

Pages précédentes : Les murs de la cage d'escalier servent de galerie d'art, avec des œuvres aussi diverses que le portrait de Robert Mapplethorpe par Andy Warhol et celui d'Angela Davis crucifiée par Peter Saul. Le papier peint géométrique des années 1970 vient de Belgique.
Page de gauche : Les murs et le plafond du vestibule sont tapissés de miroirs, ajoutant encore à l'impression d'abondance décorative. Dans le séjour, une petite culotte de John Kacere domine un tapis de Frank Stella.

Vorhergehende Seiten: Unterschiedliche Werke an der Wand des Treppenhauses wie Andy Warhols Porträt von Robert Mapplethorpe und Peter Sauls Darstellung der gekreuzigten afro-amerikanischen Aktivistin Angela Davis; die geometrisch gemusterte Tapete aus den 1970ern stammt aus Belgien.
Gegenüberliegende Seite: Verspiegelte Wände und Decke im Foyer reflektieren die fast unendliche Fülle des Dekors. Im Wohnzimmer: Ein „Unterhosen"-Gemälde von John Kacere und ein geknüpfter Teppich von Frank Stella.

En 2004, l'architecte Jonathan Leitersdorf a converti une ancienne usine à chapeaux de dix étages à NoHo en une série de lofts de 465 mètres carrés, se réservant le dernier niveau auquel il a encore ajouté un penthouse en duplex de 325 mètres carrés. Il a décoré ce dernier dans un style épuré et moderniste et l'appelle « sa maison d'été ». En effet, il s'ouvre sur une terrasse avec pelouse et, on n'ose le croire, une piscine de neuf mètres de long. (Rendue possible grâce à la citerne nécessaire au système anti-incendie de l'usine). « La maison d'hiver se trouve plus bas », explique-t-il en faisant allusion au loft original. Ce dernier est aménagé de façon plus traditionnelle, si vos traditions incluent une énorme cheminée belge du 16e siècle en pierre et d'immenses portes-fenêtres en acajou s'ouvrant, à la parisienne, sur des balcons en fer forgé.

Jonathan Leitersdorf

In 2004, Jonathan Leitersdorf, an architect, converted a 10-story former hat factory in NoHo into 5,000-square-foot floor-through lofts, retaining the top one for himself. Leitersdorf added another 3,500 square feet in the form of a two-level penthouse, which he designed in a clean, modernist style. "I call it the summer home," he says, since it opens onto a grassed terrace and, incredibly, a 30-foot-long swimming pool – "only possible because of the existing water-storage tank for the factory's sprinkler system," he explains. "The winter home is downstairs," he adds, referring to the triplex's original loft space, which is decorated in a traditional style – that is, if your traditions include a huge 16th-century Belgian stone fireplace and floor-to-ceiling mahogany-and-glass doors opening, Paris-fashion, onto wrought iron balconies.

Der Architekt Jonathan Leitersdorf verwandelte 2004 eine ehemalige, zehnstöckige Hutfabrik in NoHo in durchgehende 465-Quadratmeter-Lofts. Das Loft in der obersten Etage behielt er gleich für sich selbst. Auf dieses ließ Leitersdorf noch ein zweistöckiges schnörkellos-modernes 325 Quadratmeter großes Penthouse bauen. „Mein Sommerhaus", sagt er mit Blick auf die begrünte Terrasse und dem ganze neun Meter langen Swimmingpool, der hier nur wegen „der alten Wassertanks für die Sprinkleranlage der Fabrik eingebaut werden konnte". Das Originalloft in der unteren Etage nennt Leitersdorf entsprechend „das Winterhaus". Das Triplex-Apartment als Ganzes ist eher traditionell eingerichtet, wenn man einen belgischen Steinkamin aus dem 16. Jahrhundert und wandhohe Durchgangstüren im Pariser Stil aus Mahagoni und Glas, die auf schmiedeeiserne Balkone führen, dazuzählen möchte.

Previous pages: *The two-level brick penthouse, which Leitersdorf calls the summer home, is a new modernist addition to the building.*
Above: *The swimming pool replaced a water-storage tank for the original factory's sprinkler system.*
Right: *There are several terraces off the new penthouse.*

Pages précédentes : *Le penthouse en duplex, que Leitersdorf appelle sa maison d'été, est une extension en briques du bâtiment original.*
En haut : *La piscine a remplacé la citerne qui alimentait le système d'extinction automatique des incendies de l'usine.*
À droite : *Le nouveau penthouse possède plusieurs terrasses.*

Vorhergehende Seiten: *Das zweistöckige Backstein-Penthouse ist eine nachträgliche Ergänzung. Leitersdorf nennt es das Sommerhaus.*
Oben: *Der ehemalige Wassertank der Sprinkleranlage für die Hutfabrik wurde durch einen Swimmingpool ersetzt.*
Rechts: *Das Penthouse verfügt über mehrere Terrassen.*

Right: One of the penthouse bedrooms has its own grassed and landscaped terrace.
Below: A large entertainment area, known as the ballroom, is on the lower level of the summer home.

À droite : Une des chambres du penthouse a sa propre terrasse paysagée avec pelouse.
En bas : Au niveau inférieur du penthouse, une grande pièce de réception, baptisée la salle de bal.

Rechts: Zum Schlafzimmer im Penthouse gehört eine begrünte Terrasse.
Unten: Der untere Teil des Sommerhauses dient als Aufenthaltsraum und wird auch Ballsaal genannt.

Above: Leitersdorf calls the original loft level, the winter home.
Right: The decoration throughout the triplex is boldly masculine.
Facing page: The tin ceilings and dark-wood floors are new construction, as is the staircase to the summer home.
Following pages: The loft has across-floor vistas. The breakfast area in the kitchen has an Indian table and Balinese chairs.

En haut : Leitersdorf appelle le premier niveau, correspondant au loft original, sa maison d'hiver.
À droite : Dans tout le triplex, le décor est résolument masculin.
Page de droite : Les plafonds en métalliques et les planchers en bois sombre sont nouveaux, tout comme l'escalier menant aux quartiers d'été.
Pages suivantes : On peut voir d'un bout à l'autre du loft. Dans la cuisine, le coin du petit déjeuner avec une table indienne et des chaises balinaises.

Oben: Leitersdorf nennt die ursprüngliche Etage des Triplex in der unteren Ebene das Winterhaus.
Rechts: Die Inneneinrichtung des Lofts wirkt maskulin.
Gegenüberliegende Seite: Die Blechdecken, die dunklen Holzböden und die Treppe im Sommerhaus sind alles neue Einbauten.
Folgende Seiten: Die Blickachse geht durch das gesamte Loft; ein Tisch aus Indien mit Stühlen aus Bali in der Frühstücksecke der Küche.

New New York Interiors   Jonathan Leitersdorf

Facing page: The 16th-century stone fireplace in the living area was imported from Belgium. The leather armchairs were purchased in France.
Above: A pair of antique double doors from India connects the master bedroom to the bathroom.
Right: Kitchen countertops are made of Brazilian marble.

Page de gauche : Dans le séjour, la cheminée du 16ᵉ siècle en pierre a été importée de Belgique. Les fauteuils en cuir ont été achetés en France.
En haut : Une porte ancienne provenant d'Inde relie la chambre principale à la salle de bain.
À droite : Le comptoir de la cuisine est en marbre brésilien.

Gegenüberliegende Seite: Der Steinkamin aus dem 16. Jahrhundert kommt aus Belgien, die Ledersessel sind aus Frankreich.
Oben: Eine antike Doppeltür aus Indien verbindet das große Schlafzimmer mit dem Bad.
Rechts: Die Oberfläche der Küchentheke ist aus brasilianischem Marmor.

Quand le restaurateur et hôtelier Sean MacPherson a acheté cette maison construite en 1849, ce n'était plus qu'une carcasse inhabitable ravagée par le feu et l'eau. Venant de la côte ouest, on aurait pu s'attendre à ce qu'il fasse ressurgir des cendres un intérieur moderniste. Il a préféré s'inspirer du vieux New York qui a vu naître son bâtiment. Les pièces reconstruites sont remplies de meubles confortables et joliment délabrés qui semblent être là depuis des générations : un sofa victorien matelassé, une bergère à moitié tapissée, une table usée entourée de chaises dépareillées. MacPherson a l'art de créer des environnements patinés par le temps. Il est l'auteur des décors atemporels du Waverly Inn, de la Lafayette House, de l'hôtel Bowery et d'autres lieux branchés new-yorkais dont il est copropriétaire. Le surplus de meubles de ces établissements chics finit souvent dans sa demeure sans prétention.

Sean MacPherson

When Sean MacPherson bought his 1849 house, it was a fire-and-water damaged butchery needing a gut renovation to make habitable. MacPherson, a restaurateur and hotelier, was a West Coast transplant, so you might expect him to create a modernist home out of the ashes. Instead, he channeled the three-story building's origins in Old New York. The reconstructed rooms are filled with comfortable but genteelly shabby furniture of disparate provenance – a Victorian tufted sofa, a semi-upholstered wing chair, a timeworn dining table with mismatched chairs – that looks as if it had been amassed over generations. MacPherson has experience conjuring environments with an instant patina: He created the been-there-forever décor at the Waverly Inn, Lafayette House, The Bowery Hotel, and other hip New York properties he co-owns, and overflow furniture from those chic establishments often ends up in his unpretentious home.

Sean MacPherson kaufte dieses Haus, eine ehemalige Metzgerei, Baujahr 1849, mit Feuer- und Wasserschäden. Es benötigte eine komplette Sanierung, um überhaupt bewohnbar zu werden. Der Hotel- und Gastronomieunternehmer stammt von der Westküste, und man könnte meinen, er hätte deswegen eine besondere Vorliebe für Modernistisches. Doch er entschied sich für die Erhaltung des ursprünglichen Charakters des dreistöckigen „Old New York"-Hauses. Die restaurierten Räume sind voller bequemer, vornehm-schäbiger Möbel unterschiedlichster Herkunft: ein viktorianisches Sofa, ein nur halb bezogener Ohrensessel, ein abgenutzter Esstisch mit verschiedenen Stühlen – alles Objekte, die aussehen, als wären sie über Generationen hinweg angesammelt worden. MacPherson kennt sich mit schnell hingezauberter Patina aus: Er ist der Gründer und Mitbesitzer angesagter New Yorker Lokale und Hotels wie das Waverly Inn, das Lafayette House und das Bowery, die bereits bei ihrer Eröffnung den Eindruck erweckten, sie seien schon immer da gewesen. Und was dort keinen Platz findet, kommt häufig einfach in MacPhersons unprätentiöses Haus.

Avant d'acheter tout un étage d'une ancienne imprimerie donnant sur le luxuriant cimetière de Mulberry Street, le producteur de textiles Michael Maharam menait une existence nomade, vivant d'hôtels en restaurants. Le cabinet Architects Fernlund + Logan y a mis bon ordre en créant la demeure « idéale pour deux », à savoir lui et sa femme Sabine, peintre. Un dédale de dix-huit cellules a été abattu, les sols en béton – inclinés pour laisser s'écouler l'encre des presses – ont été remplacés par du parquet en pin douglas ou des dalles de marbre. Les détails décoratifs de la grande baignoire antique en marbre ont été poncés pour la moderniser. La plupart des meubles appartiennent à la première vague moderniste européenne et sont dignes d'un musée. « Il n'y a probablement pas plus de cinq kilos de plastique dans tout l'appartement », déclare Maharam.

Sabine & Michael Maharam

Before purchasing a floor in a former printing works with views of the churchyards on Mulberry Street, textile producer Michael Maharam was a self-described nomad. Fernlund + Logan Architects ended all that by demolishing a warren of 18 haphazard cells in his new home, creating a "one-bedroom two-person experience" for Maharam and his wife, Sabine, a painter. Old concrete floors, which sloped to drain ink spilled when the loft was filled with presses, have been replaced with new Douglas fir planks and slabs of marble. Decorative details on a large antique marble tub were ground away, modernizing it. The loft's furnishings are mostly early European modernist and mostly of museum quality. "There probably aren't ten pounds of plastic in the entire apartment," Maharam says.

Bevor der Textilhersteller Michael Maharam eine Etage mit Blick ins Grüne auf der Mulberry Street in einer ehemaligen Druckerei erwarb, lebte er wie ein Nomade, als „einer dieser Hotel- und Restaurant-Junkies". Mit der Unterstützung von Fernlund + Logan Architects beendete er dieses Dasein. Die Architekten durchbrachen eine Ansammlung 18 kleiner zusammengewürfelter Räume und machten daraus für Maharam und seine Frau Sabine, eine Malerin, einen großzügigen Wohnbereich mit einem Schlafzimmer. Auf den alten mit Druckertinte vollgesogenen Betonböden wurden Holzdielen oder Marmorplatten wie etwa im Badezimmer verlegt. Dort steht auch eine modern aussehende Marmorwanne. Tatsächlich ist es ein antikes Stück, das von allen dekorativen Details befreit wurde. Eingerichtet ist das Loft hauptsächlich mit frühen europäischen Modernisten – fast alles von Museumsqualität. Maharam: „Ich schätze, bei uns sind im gesamten Apartment keine fünf Kilo Kunststoff zu finden."

Previous pages: *A 1970s beryllium "Sonambient" sound sculpture by Harry Bertoia guards the office alcove with its Chris Lehrecke desk, Jean Prouvé chairs, and Piero Fornasetti trash can.*
Above: *The hardwood kitchen island and cabinets are built of teak.*
Right: *Different stools surround the kitchen island: a vintage "Ulmer Hocker" stool by Max Bill; a Corbusier multipurpose box from his Maison du Brésil; and the three-legged stool by Børge Mogensen.*

Pages précédentes : *« Sonambient », une sculpture sonore en béryllium d'Harry Bertoia, datant des années 1970, monte la garde devant le coin bureau, avec une table de travail de Chris Lehrecke, des chaises de Jean Prouvé et une corbeille de Piero Fornasetti.*
En haut : *L'îlot de cuisine et les placards sont en teck.*
À droite : *Autour de l'îlot de cuisine, un assortiment de tabourets : un « Ulmer Hocker » de Max Bill, une boîte polyvalente de Le Corbusier provenant de sa Maison du Brésil et un trépied de Børge Mogensen.*

Vorhergehende Seiten: *Die „Sound"-Skulptur „Sonambient" aus Beryllium von Harry Bertoia aus den 1970ern steht vor der Büroecke mit einem Tisch von Chris Lehrecke, Stühlen von Jean Prouvé und einem Papierkorb von Piero Fornasetti.*
Oben: *Die Kücheninsel und -schränke sind aus Teakholz gefertigt.*
Rechts: *Vor der Kücheninsel verstreut: ein Vintage-„Ulmer Hocker" von Max Bill; eine Mehrzweckkiste aus dem Maison du Brésil von Le Corbusier; und ein dreibeiniger Hocker von Børge Mogensen.*

Right: New softwood floors throughout the apartment are Douglas fir heartwood with exceptionally straight grain.
Below: Vintage wood chairs by Gerrit Rietveld are scattered through the apartment.

À droite : Dans tout l'appartement, les planchers sont en duramen de pin douglas au grain exceptionnellement droit.
En bas : Des chaises vintage en bois de Gerrit Rietveld sont éparpillées dans tout l'appartement.

Rechts: Die neuen Kiefernholzböden mit außergewöhnlich regelmäßiger Maserung ziehen sich durchs ganze Apartment.
Unten: Vintage-Stühle aus Holz von Gerrit Rietveld sind in der ganzen Wohnung verteilt.

Previous pages: The Alexander Girard striped "Mexicotton" fabric on the pillows was found in the archives of an architect in Holland, Michigan.
Right: Gerrit Rietveld's oak "Steltman" chair sits with rare steel-and-aluminum Jean Prouvé chairs.
Below: Beni Ouarain Berber rugs in the living area recall those in Alvar Aalto's residence. The leather-and-oak "Hunting" chairs are by Børge Mogensen, and the sculpture against the wall is by Alexandre Noll.

Pages précédentes : Le « Mexicotton » rayé d'Alexander Girard des coussins a été retrouvé dans les archives d'un architecte à Holland, dans le Michigan.
À droite : Une chaise « Steltman » en chêne de Gerrit Rietveld côtoie des chaises rares en acier et aluminium de Jean Prouvé.
En bas : Dans le coin séjour, les tapis berbères de Beni Ouarain rappellent ceux de la résidence d'Alvar Aalto. Les chaises « Hunting » en cuir et chêne sont de Børge Mogensen. La sculpture contre le mur est d'Alexandre Noll.

Vorhergehende Doppelseite: Kissenüberzüge aus gestreiftem „Mexicotton"-Stoff von Alexander Girard. Er stammt aus dem Archiv eines Architekten in Holland, Michigan.
Rechts: Ein „Steltman"-Stuhl aus Eichenholz von Gerrit Rietveld und seltene Stühle aus Stahl und Aluminium von Jean Prouvé.
Unten: Beni-Ouarain-Berberteppiche im Wohnbereich sollen an diejenigen im Haus von Alvar Aalto erinnern. Die „Hunting"-Sessel aus Leder und Eiche sind von Børge Mogensen. Vor der Wand steht eine Skulptur von Alexandre Noll.

Above: The adjustable-height pendant in the dining room is vintage Hans Wegner, paired with dining chairs by Finn Juhl.
Right: A Rietveld chair is stripped to its original yellow-accented gray.

En haut : Le plafonnier réglable dans la salle à manger est de Hans Wegner. Autour de la table, des chaises de Finn Juhl.
À droite : Un fauteuil de Rietveld a retrouvé son gris jaune d'origine.

Oben: Die höhenverstellbare Hängelampe im Essbereich von Hans Wegner gepaart mit Stühlen von Finn Juhl.
Rechts: Bei dem Rietveld-Stuhl wurden die ursprünglichen Grau- und Gelbtöne freigelegt.

Facing page: A freeform bench with Ted Muehling candlesticks sits near the master bathroom's modernized antique marble tub.
Above: In the bedroom, a Gino Sarfatti floor lamp stands beside tufted benches by Kaare Klint. The painting above them is by American artist Doris Lee.
Right: Bedroom and bathroom connect through a pocket door.

Page de gauche : Dans un coin de la salle de bain principale, avec sa baignoire en marbre modernisée, des bougeoirs de Ted Muehling sur un banc courbe.
En haut : Dans la chambre, un lampadaire de Gino Sarfatti près de banquettes capitonnées de Kaare Klint. Au-dessus, une toile de l'américaine Doris Lee.
À droite : La chambre et la salle de bain communiquent par une porte coulissante escamotable.

Gegenüberliegende Seite: Im großen Badezimmer stehen Kerzenhalter von Ted Muehling auf der organisch geformten Bank in der Nähe der modernisierten antiken Marmorbadewanne.
Oben: Stehlampe von Gino Sarfatti neben genoppten Sitzbänken von Kaare Klint. Das Bild darüber ist ein Werk der amerikanischen Künstlerin Doris Lee.
Rechts: Eine Schiebetür verbindet Schlaf- und Badezimmer.

La styliste Mary McFadden a déclaré que ses fameuses robes plissées était conçues afin que « le tissu coule sur le corps comme de l'or liquide ». En peignant au pochoir les murs et les plafonds de son appartement du Upper East Side de motifs byzantins à la feuille d'or, McFadden, qui a fermé sa maison de couture en 2002, s'est créé un environnement aussi resplendissant que le précieux métal en fusion. C'est un écrin chatoyant pour sa collection d'art, de meubles et de textiles venus des quatre coins du globe et datant du temps des pharaons à nos jours. On y retrouve les mêmes influences historiques et ethnographiques que dans ses défilés – grecques, étrusques, celtes, précolombiennes, indiennes, africaines et bien d'autres encore – le tout s'harmonisant merveilleusement grâce à l'œil expert de la maîtresse de maison, sensible à la beauté et à la puissance de l'objet créé.

Mary McFadden

Couturier Mary McFadden has said that the effect she intended with her signature pleated gowns was "of fabric falling like liquid gold on the body." By stenciling the ceilings and walls of her Upper East Side apartment with gold-leaf Byzantine motifs, the designer, who closed her fashion house in 2002, has created an environment that glows like precious molten metal. It's a lambent setting for McFadden's collection of art, furniture, and textiles, from the time of the Pharaohs to the present, and from a globe's worth of countries and cultures. The disparate array represents the same historical and ethnographic influences – Greek, Etruscan, Celtic, Pre-Columbian, Indian, African, and many more – that inspired McFadden's fashion collections, and it all works together thanks to the designer's informed eye, which responds to the beauty and power of created objects.

Mary McFadden wurde durch ihre Couture-Plisseekleider bekannt. Ihre Vorliebe erklärt sie so: „Plissierter Stoff legt sich wie flüssiges Gold um den Körper." Wie flüssiges Edelmetall glänzt auch ihr Apartment an der Upper East Side. Die Wände hat die Designerin, die ihr Modehaus 2002 aufgab, mit byzantinischen Motiven aus schabloniertem Blattgold verziert. Hier kommen McFaddens Kunstsammlung, ihre Möbel und Textilien aus verschiedenen Kulturen und Epochen – von der Pharaonenzeit bis zeitgenössisch – besonders schön zur Geltung. Die griechischen, etruskischen, keltischen, präkolumbischen, indischen, afrikanischen und anderen historischen und ethnografischen Möbel und Objekte haben die Designerin für ihre Modekollektionen inspiriert. Gewagte Kombinationen – doch dank McFaddens geschultem Auge, das Schönheit und Kreativität schätzt, sind sie äußerst gut gelungen.

Previous pages: *Etruscan-style candlesticks, a Roman gold laurel wreath, and a Tibetan Buddha's head are displayed on a Ming console table in the living room; the large vessel is by the contemporary American ceramicist, George Timock.*
Above: *The English settee, its arms carved in the form of Sirens, is Victorian; the stools are Egyptian.*
Right: *Mary McFadden, wearing one of her classic pleated gowns, stands next to a Pre-Columbian tomb marker – one of five, the others being in the British Museum.*

Pages précédentes : *Parmi les trésors exhibés sur la console Ming du séjour, des chandeliers de style étrusque, une couronne de lauriers romaine en or et une tête de bouddha tibétain. La haute potiche moderne devant la fenêtre est du céramiste américain George Timock.*
En haut : *La banquette anglaise aux accoudoirs en forme de sirène est victorienne ; les tabourets sont égyptiens.*
À droite : *Mary McFadden, dans l'une de ses célèbres robes plissées, se tient devant une stèle funéraire précolombienne. Il y en a cinq, les quatre autres se trouvant au British Museum.*

Vorhergehende Seiten: *Ausgestellte Schätze auf einem Ming-Konsolentisch im Wohnzimmer: Kerzenständer im etruskischen Stil, ein römischer Lorbeerkranz aus Gold und ein tibetischer Buddha-Kopf; das große Gefäß im Fenster stammt vom zeitgenössischen Keramikkünstler George Timock.*
Oben: *An der englischen, viktorianischen Couch dienen Sirenen als Armlehnen, die Hocker sind aus Ägypten.*
Rechts: *Mary McFadden, hier in einem ihrer klassischen Plissee-Gewänder, neben einer präkolumbischen Grabmarkierung, die zu einer Fünferserie gehört. Die anderen vier befinden sich im British Museum.*

Right: An antique Japanese Buddhist robe hangs on the bedroom wall.
Below: A 16th-century German chandelier that belonged to McFadden's mother hangs before a Byzantine-inspired set of tiered mirrors created by the designer – "Totally fake," she says, with a laugh. The tall 16th-century side chair is Syrian.

À droite : Sur un mur de la chambre, une ancienne tunique bouddhiste japonaise.
En bas : Un lustre allemand du 16ᵉ siècle, qui appartenait à la mère de McFadden, est suspendu devant un assemblage de miroirs d'inspiration byzantine créé par la styliste. « 100% toc », avoue-t-elle en riant. La chaise à haut dossier est syrienne et date du 16ᵉ siècle.

Rechts: An der Wand des Schlafzimmers ein antikes japanisches Buddhistengewand.
Unten: Der Leuchter aus dem 16. Jahrhundert stammt aus Deutschland und gehörte Mary McFaddens Mutter. Dahinter übereinander angeordnete Spiegel, die die Designerin entworfen hat. „Nichts Wertvolles", lacht sie. Der hohe Stuhl ohne Armlehnen aus dem 16. Jahrhundert ist aus Syrien.

Facing page: *McFadden designed the macramé-trimmed cloth on the dining table as well as the fabric upholstering the 16th-century Dutch chairs. As in all the rooms, the ceiling and walls are stenciled in gold to evoke the interiors of the great Byzantine basilicas. An 18th-century Austrian princess's diamond-and-ruby tiara is displayed on the wall, while the mirror is Swedish.*

Page de droite : *McFadden a dessiné le jeté de table avec une bordure en macramé ainsi que le tissu tapissant les chaises hollandaises du 16ᵉ siècle. Comme dans toutes les pièces, le plafond et les murs sont ornés de motifs dorés au pochoir pour évoquer l'intérieur d'une basilique byzantine. La tiare en rubis et diamants d'une princesse autrichienne du 18ᵉ siècle a été posée sur une applique. Le miroir est suédois.*

Gegenüberliegende Seite: *Das mit Makramee eingefasste Tuch auf dem Esstisch und der Stoff auf den holländischen Stühlen aus dem 16. Jahrhundert hat McFadden entworfen. Die Wände und die Zimmerdecken sind in jedem der Räume mit schablonierten Goldmotiven verziert. Dadurch entsteht ein Interieur so großartig wie in einer byzantinischen Basilika. An der Wand: Ein mit Diamanten und Rubinen besetztes Diadem einer österreichischen Prinzessin aus dem 18. Jahrhundert wurde zur Wandlampe umfunktioniert. Der Spiegel ist aus Schweden.*

Above: *A collection of miscellaneous objects sits on a fine Korean cabinet decorated with brass filigree.*
Right: *An elaborately carved Syrian chair, inlaid with ivory, sits in front of a 16th-century Indian scroll painting. The contemporary American ceramic vessel, filled with heads of papyrus, stands near a 16th-century Russian icon.*

En haut : *Une collection disparate d'objets posés sur un beau cabinet coréen orné de filigranes de cuivre.*
À droite : *Derrière un siège syrien, sculpté et orné d'incrustations en ivoire, un rouleau indien du 16ᵉ siècle. La potiche moderne en céramique, remplie de papyrus, est posée près d'une icône russe du 16ᵉ siècle.*

Oben: *Verschiedene Objekte auf einem koreanischen Schrank mit filigranen Verzierungen aus Messing.*
Rechts: *Ein aufwendig geschnitzter syrischer Stuhl mit Einlegearbeiten vor einem Rollbild aus Indien aus dem 16. Jahrhundert. Auf dem Boden hinter dem zeitgenössischen amerikanischen mit Papyrushalmen gefüllten Keramikgefäß steht eine russische Ikone aus dem 16. Jahrhundert.*

New New York Interiors   Mary McFadden

Le loft spectaculaire de Lee Mindel est perché au sommet d'une ancienne usine à chapeaux dans le quartier du Flatiron. « Les travaux ont été un vrai casse-tête, tant structurel que mécanique », avoue-t-il. Pour mener à bien la tache ardue, son cabinet d'architecture, Shelton, Mindel & Associates, s'est associé à celui de Reed A. Morrison. Pour pallier le manque de fenêtres, dix grandes ouvertures ont été percées dans les murs en maçonnerie afin de faire entrer la lumière et de jouir de vues panoramiques. Désormais, on ne peut plus douter que Manhattan soit une île car, nous dit Mindel, « d'un côté on voit le Hudson et de l'autre, East River ». Dans la nouvelle rotonde de l'entrée, le grand escalier en colimaçon en acier et béton de Mindel mène à un salon solarium ceint de verre. La structure claire et spacieuse rappelle la citerne voisine sur le toit ou, selon le maître des lieux, la couronne de la Statue de la Liberté.

Lee Mindel

Architect Lee Mindel's spectacular loft occupies what was the dark top floor of a Flatiron District hatmaker. "It was very tough to build, both structurally and mechanically," says Mindel, whose firm, Shelton, Mindel & Associates, collaborated with Reed A. Morrison Architect on the difficult job. The space had few windows, so the architects broke ten large ones through the masonry walls to bring in light and panoramic views. Now, being in the apartment, "you understand that Manhattan is an island because you can see the Hudson and the East rivers," Mindel says. The new entry rotunda is wrapped by Mindel's "double-helix" stainless steel and concrete staircase, which leads to a glass-enclosed solarium lounge. The airy structure echoes the shape of the adjacent rooftop water tower, though Mindel admits it also recalls the crown on the Statue of Liberty.

Das spektakuläre Loft des Architekten Lee Mindel liegt im obersten Stockwerk einer ehemaligen Hutmanufaktur im Flatiron District. Für den Umbau arbeitete Mindels Firma Shelton, Mindel & Associates mit dem Architekten Reed A. Morrison zusammen. „Ein schwieriges Unterfangen, strukturell wie auch mechanisch", sagt Mindel im Rückblick. Die Räume waren düster, hatten kaum Fenster. Um Licht und Ausblick zu schaffen, brachen die Architekten zehn große Fenster aus den Mauern. Mindel: „Nun blickt man auf den Hudson und den East River, und man kann erkennen, dass Manhattan eine Insel ist." In der neuen Eingangsrotunde führt eine „Doppelhelix"-Treppe aus Edelstahl und Beton, von Mindel entworfen, aufs Dach in die verglaste Solarium-Lounge. Die luftige Konstruktion spiegelt die Form des nahe gelegenen Wassertanks wider, obschon Mindel sagt, sie erinnere ihn auch an den Strahlenkranz der Freiheitsstatue.

Previous pages: A rooftop solarium addition echoes the form of
the building's water tower.
Facing page: An early Tom Dixon table with a chromed wire base
stands in the entrance rotunda.
Above: A seating group, including a Frits Henningsen armchair, is
lighted by a Flos wall lamp, a Fontana Arte table lamp, and floor
lamp by Serge Mouille.
Right: Mindel stands next to a Poul Kjærholm leather daybed in
his living room.

Pages précédentes : Le solarium sur le toit rappelle la forme de
la citerne de l'immeuble.
Page de gauche : Dans la rotonde de l'entrée, une table de Tom
Dixon avec un pied en fil de fer chromé, une œuvre de ses débuts.
En haut : Ce coin salon, qui inclut un fauteuil de Frits Henningsen,
est éclairé avec une applique de Flos, une lampe de Fontana Arte
et un lampadaire de Serge Mouille.
À droite : Mindel dans son séjour, derrière un lit de repos de Poul
Kjærholm.

Vorhergehende Seiten: Das Solarium auf dem Dach spiegelt die Form
des Wassertanks auf dem Gebäude wider.
Gegenüberliegende Seite: Ein Frühwerk von Tom Dixon: der Tisch
mit verchromtem Drahtgestell in der Eingangsrotunde.
Oben: Eine Wandlampe von Flos, eine Tischlampe von Fontana Arte
und eine Stehlampe von Serge Mouille beleuchten die Sitzgruppe,
darunter ein Sessel von Frits Henningsen.
Rechts: Mindel hinter einer Liege von Poul Kjærholm.

Above: Small bulbs have been fitted into the bobèches of the Lobmeyr candle chandelier above the dining table.
Right: A re-edition of an Antoni Gaudí bench is adjacent to the stainless steel and concrete "double-helix" stair.
Facing page: The living room fireplace has a surround made of structural-glass framed with stainless steel and a Jean Prouvé table.
Following pages: A pair of vintage Hans Wegner "Ox" chairs sits near one of the ten new windows created in the loft. A French Cubist plaster maquette rises on the corner table.

En haut : De petites ampoules ont été vissées dans les bobèches du chandelier de Lobmeyr au-dessus de la table de salle à manger.
À droite : Au pied de l'escalier en « double hélice » en acier inoxydable et béton, une réédition d'un banc d'Antoni Gaudí.
Page de droite : Dans le séjour, une cheminée dont le manteau est en briques creuses et acier inoxydable. Au milieu de la pièce, une table de Jean Prouvé.
Pages suivantes : Une paire de fauteuils « Ox » de Hans Wegner devant l'une des dix nouvelles fenêtres créées dans le loft. Sur l'une des tables d'appoint, une sculpture cubiste française en plâtre.

Oben: Über dem Esstisch ein Kerzenleuchter von Lobmeyr. Anstelle von Kerzen sind in den Manschetten nun kleine Glühbirnen.
Rechts: Neben der „Doppelhelix"-Treppe aus Edelstahl und Beton die Neuauflage einer Bank von Antoni Gaudí.
Gegenüberliegende Seite: Der Kamin im Wohnzimmer mit Bauglas und Edelstahleinfassung. Der Tisch ist von Jean Prouvé.
Folgende Seiten: Zwei „Ox"-Sessel von Hans Wegner flankieren eines der zehn neu eingebauten Loftfenster. Auf dem Beistelltisch in der Ecke steht eine kubistische Gipsskulptur aus Frankreich.

La collection de design moderniste de Julianne Moore méritait d'être mise en valeur dans un environnement dépouillé. Aussi, quand, en 2001, la comédienne a confié aux architectes de MADE la rénovation de son loft dans le West Village, elle a demandé beaucoup d'espace de rangement. MADE, co-fondé par son beau-frère Oliver Freundlich, a trouvé une solution architecturale : un placard en chêne assez haut pour faire cloison entre la cuisine et le bureau, et suffisamment profond pour y cacher tout un bric-à-brac. La structure a été mise à nu puis réorganisée en un espace fluide délimité par des groupements de meubles, des photos et quelques éléments robustes. Moore et son époux Bart ont été tellement séduits qu'ils ont demandé à MADE de s'attaquer à leur nouvelle maison construite en 1840.

Julianne Moore & Bart Freundlich

Julianne Moore's modernist design collection looks best in a clutter-free setting. So when the actress instructed her architects, MADE, on the 2001 renovation of her West Village loft, "I asked for great storage space," she says. MADE, co-founded by Moore's brother-in-law, Oliver Freundlich, turned the request for stowage into an architectural statement: a freestanding oak cabinet between kitchen and study, tall enough to be a partition, and deep enough to hide a lot of paraphernalia. The apartment was stripped back to its bones, and then reorganized as flowing space demarcated with furniture groupings, photographic works, and architectural elements. Moore and her husband Bart so liked MADE's design that they hired the firm to renovate the townhouse the family recently moved to.

Julianne Moores Sammlung moderner Designerobjekte kommt in einer schlichten, ordentlichen Umgebung am schönsten zur Geltung. „Ich brauche vor allem viel Stauraum", sagte deshalb die Schauspielerin zu den Architekten von MADE, die 2001 ihr Loft im West Village umbauten. Oliver Freundlich, Moores Schwager und Mitbegründer von MADE, machte daraus ein elegantes architektonisches Statement: Ein großer frei stehender Schrank aus Eiche zwischen Küche und Büro dient einerseits als Raumtrenner und bietet gleichzeitig genug Stauraum für Kleinkram. Die Räumlichkeiten wurden bis auf ihre industriellen Grundelemente freigelegt und zu einem offenen Apartment umgebaut. Einzig Möbelgruppen, Fotografien und Einbauten wie der frei stehende Schrank strukturieren den Raum. Die Umsetzung von MADE begeisterte Moore und ihren Mann Bart Freundlich derart, dass sie die Architekten wieder für die Renovierung eines Stadthauses, in das die Familie kürzlich gezogen ist, beauftragten.

Previous pages: MADE exposed the loft's industrial bones, like the original pine columns and beams, and stained the floors a unifying ebony. The living area is demarcated by the furniture, which includes Vladimir Kagan sectional sofas and a George Nakashima coffee table.
Above: The study, separated from the kitchen by an oak storage partition, is a space the family naturally gravitates to.
Right: A handsome display case for ceramics helps delineate the living and dining areas.

Pages précédentes : MADE a mis à nu la structure industrielle originale du bâtiment, avec ses poutres et colonnes en pin, puis a teint tous les planchers couleur d'ébène. Le séjour est délimité par l'agencement des meubles, qui incluent un canapé modulaire de Vladimir Kagan et une table basse de George Nakashima.
En haut : Le bureau, séparé de la cuisine par un haut placard en chêne, est un lieu vers lequel gravitent naturellement tous les membres de la famille.
À droite : Un beau meuble à compartiments rempli de céramiques sépare la salle à manger du séjour.

Vorhergehende Seiten: MADE legte zunächst die Grundstruktur des industriellen Lofts frei. Dabei kamen Säulen und Balken aus Kiefer zum Vorschein. Die Böden wurden einheitlich in einem Ebenholzton gebeizt. Das Wohnzimmer ist mit Möbeln aus Moores umfangreicher Sammlung eingerichtet – darunter ein Sofasystem von Vladimir Kagan und ein Couchtisch von George Nakashima.
Oben: Ein Eichenschrank grenzt das Büro von der Küche ab. Hier hält sich die Familie am liebsten auf.
Rechts: Das schöne Schauregal mit Keramikobjekten markiert den Übergang vom Essraum zum Wohnzimmer.

Right: Moore had always wanted a laboratory-style stainless-steel kitchen. MADE used a dropped ceiling to define the kitchen's work area.
Below: The stainless-steel kitchen counter is cantilevered four feet into the public space; the stools are by Jean Prouvé. MADE designed an elegant new staircase with open treads, side panels of stainless-steel mesh, and a Hermès-like leather handrail.

À droite : Moore avait toujours rêvé d'une cuisine laboratoire toute en acier. MADE a abaissé le plafond pour délimiter l'espace cuisine.
En bas : Le comptoir de la cuisine saille de plus d'un mètre dans l'espace commun. Les tabourets sont de Jean Prouvé. MADE a conçu l'élégant escalier en acier sans contremarches et avec une rampe en cuir à la Hermès.

Rechts: Eine professionelle Edelstahlküche war ein lang gehegter Wunsch Moores. MADE nutzte eine abgehängte Decke, um den Arbeitsbereich der Küche räumlich zu definieren.
Unten: Die Küchenablage aus Edelstahl ragt etwa 1,5 Meter in den Wohnraum hinein; die Barhocker sind von Jean Prouvé. MADE entwarf auch die neue, elegante Treppe mit offenen Stufen, Seitenpaneelen aus Edelstahlgeflecht und einen Handlauf aus Leder im Hermès-Stil.

Facing page: Moore and her husband are also avid collectors of contemporary photography, and MADE designed some spaces, like the dining area, around specific works – in this case, a large Thomas Struth landscape that's like a window onto another world.

Page de droite : Moore et son mari sont également de fervents collectionneurs de photographie contemporaine. MADE a conçu certains espaces autour d'œuvres spécifiques comme ici, dans le coin salle à manger, où un paysage de Thomas Struth ouvre une fenêtre sur un autre monde.

Gegenüberliegende Seite: Moore und ihr Ehemann sind begeisterte Sammler zeitgenössischer Fotografie, und MADE arrangierte ein paar Räume rund um bestimmte Arbeiten wie dieses große Landschaftsbild von Thomas Struth im Essbereich. Es wirkt wie ein Fenster in eine andere Welt.

Above: The loft was intended to accommodate Moore's extensive collection of mid-century modern furniture, like this wall cabinet by Harvey Probber and console table by T.H. Robsjohn-Gibbings.
Right: The custom-made marine-grade-teak cabinetry is a warm contrast to the cool limestone of the floor and walls in the master bathroom.

En haut : Le loft a été aménagé pour accueillir la vaste collection de meubles modernistes du milieu du 20ᵉ siècle, comme ce placard d'Harvey Probber et la console de T.H. Robsjohn-Gibbings.
À droite : Dans la salle de bain principale, l'ébénisterie sur mesure en teck marin offre un contraste chaleureux avec la fraîcheur du travertin du sol et des murs.

Oben: Das Loft wurde für die große Möbelsammlung Moores aus der Mitte des 20. Jahrhunderts konzipiert. Dazu gehören dieser Wandschrank von Harvey Probber und der Konsolentisch von T. H. Robsjohn-Gibbings.
Rechts: Die maßgefertigten Schränke aus Teak sind ein warmer Kontrast zum kühlen Kalkstein am Boden und an den Wänden des großen Badezimmers.

New New York Interiors   Julianne Moore & Bart Freundlich

Pour transformer sa garçonnière dans le West Village en un foyer fonctionnel de 95 mètres carrés, le consultant en informatique Josh Morton a fait appel au cabinet LOT-EK. Ce dernier y a fait entrer une citerne de camion de 272.550 litres, ce qui était approprié puisque l'endroit était autrefois un garage de poids lourds. LOT-EK, qui s'inspire de l'industrie lourde, en a fait deux lits capsules, chacun assez grand pour accueillir un matelas à deux places. Il a fallu une grue pour les hisser dans l'appartement, puis les déposer sur une mezzanine qui enjambe lehaut espace. Une autre section de la citerne a été installée verticalement pour accueillir deux salles de bain superposées, celle du dessus étant reliée à la mezzanine par une étroite passerelle. De sa nouvelle demeure, Susan Weinthaler, l'épouse de Morton, déclare : « On s'y fait très rapidement ! »

Josh Morton & Susan Weinthaler

For the renovation of computer consultant Josh Morton's bachelor pad, architects LOT-EK bought a 72,000-gallon oil-truck tank – appropriately, since Morton's 1,000-square-foot West Village apartment is located in a former truck-parking garage. LOT-EK, which is inspired by heavy industry, transformed the tank into twin sleeping pods, each just big enough to accommodate a king-size mattress. A crane swung the pods into the apartment, where they were installed as a mezzanine bridging the high-ceilinged space. Another slice of the tank was installed vertically to house a pair of double-decker bathrooms. A narrow catwalk links the upper bathroom to the mezzanine. It's now an efficient family home; as Morton's wife, Susan Weinthaler, says, "Living here quickly seemed rather normal".

Die Architekturfirma LOT-EK erwarb für den Umbau der ehemaligen Junggesellenbude des Computer-Beraters Josh Morton den 272 550-Liter-Öltank eines Lastwagens. Und das passte ganz gut, denn Mortons 95 Quadratmeter großes Apartment im West Village liegt neben einem ehemaligen Lastwagen-Parkhaus. Die Architekten von LOT-EK, die sich oft von der Schwerindustrie inspirieren lassen, bauten in den Tank zwei Schlafzellen – jede so groß, damit gerade eine Doppelmatratze reinpasst. Die Zellen wurden mit einem Kran in das Apartment gehievt, wo sie als Zwischenetage den hohen Raum aufteilen. Ein anderes Stück des Tanks wurde vertikal eingebaut. Darin befinden sich auf zwei Ebenen übereinander die beiden Badezimmer. Nur ein schmaler Laufsteg verbindet das obere Badezimmer mit der Zwischenetage. Inzwischen hat Morten geheiratet und seine Frau, Susan Weinthaler, sagt: „Hier zu leben, erschien ganz schnell normal."

Left: Two bathrooms are installed double-decker style in an upended section of the tank.
Below: Bathroom interiors feature the same canary coloured baked-on car paint as the pods; LOT-EK named it safety yellow.

À gauche : Les deux salles de bain sont installées l'une sur l'autre dans une section verticale de la citerne.
En bas : L'intérieur des salles de bain est peint de la même laque de carrosserie jaune canari que les capsules; LOT-EK la désigne de « jaune sécurité ».

Links: Zwei Badezimmer im Doppeldeckerstil befinden sich in einem umgestülpten Teil des Tanks.
Unten: Die Badezimmer sind im selben kanarienvogelgelben Autolack, welchen LOT-EK als „Sicherheitsgelb" bezeichnet, wie das Innere der Schlafzellen gestrichen.

Previous pages: Only a narrow catwalk connects the two sleeping pods to the mezzanine bathroom. The pods have gull-wing doors on both sides that open using hydraulic pistons.
Facing page: The oil-tank mezzanine spans the entire width of the apartment over the dining area's custom resin table.

Pages précédentes : Une étroite passerelle relie les deux lits capsules à la salle de bain en mezzanine. Les capsules sont équipées de portes papillons qui s'ouvrent à l'aide d'un piston hydraulique.
Page de gauche : La mezzanine occupe toute la largeur du loft. Dessous se trouve la salle à manger, avec une table en résine réalisée sur mesure.

Vorhergehende Seiten: Der schmale Laufsteg ist die einzige Verbindung der beiden Schlafzellen mit dem Badezimmer auf der Zwischenetage. Die Türen auf beiden Seiten der Zellen erinnern an Möwenflügel, sie lassen sich hydraulisch öffnen.
Gegenüberliegende Seite: Der Öltank spannt sich als Zwischenetage über die ganze Breite des Apartments. Darunter: ein spezialgefertigter Tisch aus Kunstharz.

Julian Schnabel peint sur des toiles immenses, il était donc naturel que pour l'extension du bâtiment du West Village où il habite et travaille depuis longtemps, il voit grand. « Je voulais de l'espace pour bouger, de l'air pour respirer », explique-t-il. De fait, les neuf étages érigés sur le toit comprennent cinq immenses appartements – parmi lesquels un triplex et deux duplex (dont un qu'il occupe avec son épouse Olatz López Garmendia et leurs fils jumeaux), tandis que la partie ancienne inclut désormais un atelier, une galerie et une piscine. Avec sa façade enduite de stuc rouge Pompéi, ses fenêtres cintrées, ses balcons, ses colonnades et ses terrasses, le « Palazzo Chupi » évoque Venise, et ses intérieurs aux cheminées massives, aux hauts plafonds, aux murs stuqués et aux sols dallés ne dépareilleraient pas au bord du Grand Canal. C'est la Sérénissime sur Hudson.

Palazzo Chupi

Artist Julian Schnabel paints on a grand scale, so when expanding the century-old West Village building where he has long lived and worked, he naturally thought big. "I wanted tall ceilings, space to move, air to breathe," Schnabel says, and that's what he has conjured: an 9-story addition comprising five huge apartments – a triplex, two duplexes (one occupied by Schnabel, his wife, Olatz López Garmendia, and their twin sons), and two single-story homes – along with a studio, gallery space, and swimming pool on the lower floors. Finished in Pompeii-red stucco, and festooned with arched windows, balconies, colonnades, and terraces, Palazzo Chupi, as Schnabel has named it, evokes Venice of the doges. And with their massive fireplaces, hand-plastered walls, tiled floors, and high ceilings, the apartment interiors would look right at home on the Grand Canal, too – La Serenissima on the Hudson.

Der Künstler Julian Schnabel malt in großen Dimensionen. Bei der Erweiterung des hundertjährigen Gebäudes im West Village, in dem er seit Langem lebt, dachte er ebenso großzügig: „Ich wünschte mir hohe Räume, Bewegungsfreiheit und Luft zum Atmen!" Genau das hat er im neun Stockwerke hohen Aufbau herbeigezaubert. Darin sind fünf riesige Apartments untergebracht – darunter eine Triplex-Wohnung und zwei Duplex-Wohnungen (in der einen lebt Schnabel zusammen mit seiner Frau Olatz López Garmendia und den Zwillingssöhnen). In den unteren Geschossen befinden sich ein Atelier, eine Galerie und ein Swimmingpool. Der Palazzo Chupi, wie Schnabel das Gebäude nennt, erinnert an das Venedig der Dogen: Fassade in pompejischem Rot, Bogenfenster, Säulengänge, Zierbalkone und Terrassen. Dazu kommen riesige Kamine, von Hand verputzte Wände, Fliesenböden und hohe Räume – La Serenissima am Hudson River.

Facing page: The terrace's wall sconces, cast-stone and bronze railings, and metal-frame French doors were made specifically for the palazzo, as were most of its fixtures and fittings. The cement tiles are Moroccan; the wicker furniture is Art Deco.

Page de droite : Les appliques de la terrasse, la balustrade en simili-pierre et bronze et les portes-fenêtres métalliques ont été réalisées spécialement pour le palazzo, comme la plupart des équipements de l'extension. Le carrelage en ciment est marocain. Les meubles en osier sont Art Déco.

Gegenüberliegende Seite: Die Wandleuchter auf der Terrasse, die Geländer aus Stein und Bronze und die metallgerahmten Fenstertüren sind alle Spezialanfertigungen – wie die meisten anderen Halterungen und Einbauten auch. Die Zementfliesen am Boden stammen aus Marokko, die Korbmöbel sind Art déco.

Previous pages: Artist Julian Schnabel created Palazzo Chupi a 12-story Venetian-style apartment house from the century-old, three-story brick building that has been his studio (and, later, residence) since 1987.
Above: The balconied and colonnaded addition, which contains five large apartments, including a duplex for the Schnabel family, is finished in Pompeii-red and natural stucco.
Right: Schnabel designed the concrete-and-tile dining table on the principal terrace.

Pages précédentes : Julian Schnabel a créé le Palazzo Chupi à partir de l'immeuble en briques vieux d'un siècle qui abritait son atelier (puis sa résidence) depuis 1987, lui rajoutant douze étages décorés à la vénitienne et comptant plusieurs appartements.
En haut : L'extension, aux façades enduites de stucs naturels et rouge Pompéi et ornées de colonnades et de balcons, comprend cinq grands appartements dont un duplex pour la famille Schnabel.
À droite : Schnabel a conçu lui-même la table en béton et carrelage de la terrasse principale.

Vorherige Seiten: Das insgesamt zwölf-stöckige Apartmentgebäude wurde auf ein 100 Jahre altes, ursprünglich dreistöckiges Backsteinhaus gebaut, in dem sich seit 1987 Schnabels Atelier (und später auch seine Wohnung) befindet.
Oben: Der Aufbau im pompejischen Rot mit Balkonen, Säulengängen und Naturverputz hat fünf große Apartments, darunter die Duplex-Wohnung der Familie Schnabel.
Rechts: Den Esstisch aus Beton und Kacheln auf der großen Terrasse hat Schnabel entworfen.

Above: By using dark-stained recycled-pine clapboard for the lobby walls, Schnabel wanted to evoke a boathouse, whether for a Venetian gondola or an Adirondack canoe.
Right: The portrait is of Venetian aristocrat Count Giovanni Volpi.
Facing page: A mirror in a gilded Regency frame hangs in the elevator, which has pine-clad walls and a ceiling lined with copper. Schnabel designed the bronze-and-burlap bench.

En haut : Les murs de l'entrée sont revêtus de bardeaux en pin recyclé et teinté pour évoquer un hangar à bateaux, celui-ci pouvant abriter une gondole vénitienne ou un canoë de l'Adirondack.
À droite : Un portrait du comte Giovanni Volpi, un aristocrate vénitien.
Page de droite : Un miroir dans un cadré doré Regency est accroché dans l'ascenseur, dont les parois sont tapissées de bardeaux en pin et le plafond de cuivre. Schnabel a dessiné le banc en bronze et toile à sac.

Oben: Die Wände der Eingangshalle sind mit dunkel gebeizten Holzpaneelen verkleidet. Schnabel wollte damit Bootshaus-Atmosphäre – für eine venezianische Gondel oder ein Kanu in den Adirondacks – schaffen.
Rechts: Porträt des venezianischen Aristokraten Giovanni Volpi.
Gegenüberliegende Seite: Spiegel in einem vergoldeten Regency-Rahmen im Aufzug mit Kiefernholzauskleidung und Kupferblende. Die Bank aus Bronze und Leinengurtgeflecht ist ein Entwurf von Schnabel.

Facing page: In the main living room, a bronze floor lamp made from the toothed snout of a sawfish stands next to an 18th-century Italian daybed. Artworks include a 1933 portrait of Suzy Solidor by Francis Picabia, and a large "tarp" painting by Schnabel from 1987.
Above: With its 18-foot-high ceilings, the living room easily accommodates an enormous canvas like Schnabel's 2001 "Large Girl with No Eyes."
Right: The kitchen walls are partly covered with green terra-cotta tiles; the cast-concrete countertops are also vivid green.

Page de gauche : Dans le grand salon, un lampadaire en bronze réalisé avec le rostre d'un poisson-scie se dresse près d'un lit de repos italien du 18e siècle. Parmi les œuvres d'art, un portrait de Suzy Solidor par Francis Picabia datant de 1933 et une grande toile « bâche » de Schnabel datant de 1987.
En haut : Avec près de 5,50m de hauteur sous plafond, le salon peut accueillir des toiles monumentales comme « Large Girl with No Eyes » (2001) de Schnabel.
À droite : Les murs de la cuisine sont partiellement tapissés de carreaux en terre cuite verts. Les plans de travail en béton moulé sont également verts.

Gegenüberliegende Seite: Bronzene Bodenlampe aus einer Sägefischschnauze im großen Wohnzimmer neben einer italienischen Liege aus dem 18. Jahrhundert. Unter den Kunstwerken: ein Suzy-Solidor-Porträt von Francis Picabia, 1933, und ein großes „Tarp"-Gemälde von Schnabel, 1987.
Oben: Auch riesige Gemälde wie Schnabels „Large Girl with Eyes" von 2001 finden in den fünfeinhalb Meter hohen Räumen Platz.
Rechts: Sattes Grün: die Terrakotta-Kacheln an den Küchenwänden und die aus Beton gegossenen Arbeitsplatten.

Previous pages: Two related Schnabel canvases from 2005,
"Je ne rien" and "Fore Get Nothing," hang on either side of the living
room's massive cast-stone fireplace, which Schnabel also designed.
Facing page: Schnabel has decorated the living room of the palazzo's
triplex penthouse in the same style as his own duplex.
Above: In the triplex's master bedroom, French forties table lamps
by Serge Roche flank the headboard-a fiberglass cast that Schnabel
painted and gilded.
Right: An Italian mirror hangs above the bedroom fireplace.

Double page précédente : Deux toiles de Schnabel de 2005, sont
accrochées de part et d'autre de la cheminée massive en similipierre
du salon. Au-dessus, une photo de Luigi Ontanti.
Page de gauche : Schnabel a décoré le salon du penthouse en triplex
du palazzo dans le même style que son propre duplex.
En haut : Dans la chambre principale du triplex, des lampes de
chevet de Serge Roche flanquent la tête de lit en fibre de verre moulée,
peinte et dorée par Schnabel. La toile George Condo date de 1988.
À droite : Un miroir italien est suspendu au-dessus de la cheminée
de la chambre.

Vorherige Seiten: Gemälde von 2005 „Je ne rien" und „Fore Get
Nothing" neben dem riesigen Kunststeinkamin im Wohnzimmer.
Gegenüberliegende Seite: Schnabel hat das Wohnzimmer des
Triplex-Penthouses im gleichen Stil eingerichtet wie seine Duplex-
Wohnung.
Oben: Das Kopfteil des Betts im Schlafzimmer der Triplex-Wohnung
hat Schnabel aus Fiberglas gegossen, dann bemalt und vergoldet.
Daneben stehen französische Tischlampen aus den 1940ern von
Serge Roche. Das Gemälde stammt von George Condo, 1988.
Rechts: Ein italienischer Spiegel über dem Schlafzimmerkamin.

Above: *The master bathroom has a working fireplace. Marble tiles cover the walls and floor.*
Right: *Board-and-batten wood ceilings create a sense of warmth.*
Facing page: *In the master bedroom, two large paintings by Schnabel from 1979, flank smaller works by Joseph Beuys, Andy Warhol, and Picasso, among others. The painted and gilded wardrobe, which features stuccowork, is by Serge Roche.*
Following pages: *There is a swimming pool on the ground floor.*

En haut : *La salle de bain est équipée d'une vraie cheminée. Les murs et le sol sont tapissés de carreaux de marbre. Un miroir italien du 17ᵉ siècle est accroché au-dessus du double lavabo en porcelaine.*
À droite : *Le plafond en lattes de bois crée une atmosphère chaleureuse.*
Page de droite : *Dans la chambre principale, deux grandes toiles de Schnabel de 1979, côtoient des œuvres plus petites de Joseph Beuys, Andy Warhol et Picasso. La penderie peinte est de Serge Roche.*
Double page suivante : *Le rez-de-chaussée du bâtiment original, accueille désormais une piscine.*

Oben: *Im Kamin des Badezimmers in Schnabels Duplex-Wohnung kann man ein richtiges Feuer anzünden. Italienischer Spiegel aus dem 17. Jahrhundert über dem Porzellan-Doppelwaschbecken.*
Rechts: *Holzverkleidete Decken erzeugen eine warme Atmosphäre.*
Gegenüberliegende Seite: *Im Schlafzimmer hängen zwei grosse Bilder von Schnabel von 1979, neben kleineren Werken von Joseph Beuys, Andy Warhol, Picasso und anderen. Der Wandschrank mit Stuck ist von Serge Roche.*
Folgende Seiten: *Im Erdgeschoss befindet sich ein Swimmingpool.*

La maison atelier du peintre et sculpteur israélien Izhar Patkin dans le East Village, une partie d'une ancienne école de formation professionnelle, est aussi vaste et riche que son art narratif. Tous deux abondent en iconographie historique, religieuse et culturelle. Prenez l'installation qui occupe tout un mur de sa salle de réunion : réalisée peu après son arrivée à New York au début des années 1980, elle recourt à des techniques de trompe-l'œil pour associer des références au vieux continent, tels que Kafka et Arcimboldo, à des traditions du nouveau monde comme l'art populaire des Allemands de Pennsylvanie. Son méandre de pièces remplies de meubles provenant de tous les continents et époques offre un voyage à travers une esthétique qui recherche l'harmonie du monde. Il accorde la même importance à chaque objet, tissu et meuble et tous ont une histoire captivante à raconter.

Izhar Patkin

Painter and sculptor Izhar Patkin's enormous East Village home and studio – part of a former vocational training school – is as expansive and inclusive as the narrative-form art works he creates. There's a world's worth of historical, religious, and cultural imagery to be found in both. Take the wall-size installation in Patkin's conference room: Made soon after the Israeli-born artist came to New York in the early 1980s, it uses trompe-l'œil techniques to combine Old World references like Kafka and Arcimboldo with New World traditions like Pennsylvania-Dutch barn painting. With furnishings drawn from every continent and epoch, the seemingly numberless rooms in his home provide a vivid journey through Patkin's world-harmonizing aesthetic. Every textile, object, and piece of furniture is equally valued and has an equally compelling story to tell.

Das Wohnatelier des Malers und Bildhauers Izhar Patkin in einer ehemaligen Gesangsschule im East Village ist riesig. Typisch für Patkin: Alles wirkt großzügig und gemütlich zugleich. Und man findet eine Fülle geschichtlicher, religiöser und kultureller Bildsprachen. Wie etwa bei der wandgroßen Installation im Besprechungsraum, die der gebürtige Israeli kurz nach seiner Ankunft in New York in den frühen 1980ern schuf. In diesem Werk verbinden sich Trompe-l'œil und Referenzen an Kafka und Arcimboldo mit kunsthandwerklichen Traditionen der Neuen Welt wie der Volkskunst der sogenannten Pennsylvania-Dutch-Einwanderern aus Deutschland. Die Einrichtung ist ein Abbild von Patkins weltvereinigender Ästhetik: Möbel und Objekte stammen von diversen Kontinenten und aus verschiedensten Epochen. Jedes Stück Stoff, jeder Gegenstand und jedes Möbel nimmt dabei selbstbewusst und gleichberechtigt seinen Platz ein.

Left: The artist designed the imposing metal-and-glass double doors in the entry foyer.
Below: Patkin's friend, artist Kim MacConnel, painted the screening room's chairs and bamboo-forest curtains. Indian plastic lanterns make a torch.

À gauche : Patkin a réalisé lui-même l'imposante double porte en métal et verre du vestibule.
En bas : L'artiste Kim MacConnel, ami de Patkin, a peint les chaises et le motif de bambous des rideaux de la salle de projection. Le lampadaire a été réalisé avec des lanternes indiennes en plastique.

Links: Die imposante Doppeltür aus Metall und Glas im Eingangsfoyer ist ein Entwurf von Patkin.
Unten: Die Stühle und den Vorhang hat der befreundete Künstler Kim MacConnel bemalt. Die Lampe besteht aus indischen Plastiklaternen.

Previous pages: Bertoia chairs surround Moroccan tray tables in the shaded courtyard. Wisteria blooms on the upper deck.
Facing page: In the dressing room, Sikh wedding scarves act as curtains on built-in closets. The hanging lamp is from a Lower East Side synagogue.

Pages précédentes : Dans la cour ombragée, des chaises de Bertoia entourent des plateaux marocains montés en table. La terrasse à l'étage est envahie par la glycine.
Page de gauche : Dans le dressing, des écharpes de mariage sikhs servent de rideaux aux penderies encastrées. La lanterne provient d'une synagogue du Lower East Side.

Vorhergehende Seiten: Bertoia-Stühle um marokkanische Tische im schattigen Innenhof. Auf der oberen Terrasse blühen Glyzinien.
Gegenüberliegende Seite: Sikh-Hochzeitstücher dienen als Vorhänge vor den eingebauten Wandschränken im Ankleidezimmer. Die Deckenlampe stammt aus einer Synagoge der Lower East Side.

Above: A work based on photographs of Patkin's parents' wedding hangs over MacConnel painted furniture in the living room.
Right: The colorful chandelier in the hallway was assembled from pieces of glass left over from one of Patkin's sculptures.
Facing page: MacConnel chairs surround a recycled-wood dining table made by Nelson Perkins, who was once Fidel Castro's carpenter.

En haut : Dans le salon, une œuvre basée sur des photos de mariage des parents de Patkin est accrochée au-dessus de meubles peints par MacConnel.
À droite : Le lustre coloré dans le couloir a été réalisé avec les déchets de verre de l'une des sculptures de Patkin.
Page de droite : Des chaises peintes par MacConnel entourent une table en bois recyclé de Nelson Perkins, qui fut autrefois le menuisier de Fidel Castro.

Oben: Ein Hochzeitsfoto von Patkins Eltern diente als Vorlage für das Bild über den von MacConnel bemalten Sesseln im Wohnraum.
Rechts: Der bunte Leuchter in der Eingangshalle besteht aus Glasstückchen, die von einer Skulptur von Patkin übrig geblieben sind.
Gegenüberliegende Seite: Von MacConnel bemalte Polsterstühle stehen rund um einen Tisch aus recyceltem Holz, der von Nelson Perkins, dem ehemaligen Schreiner Fidel Castros, gefertigt wurde.

Deine
Freudensmomente
haben die
Präzision
militärischer Strategie

Facing page: Patkin made the meeting room's wall-size mixed-media installation, "Before the Law Stands a Doorkeeper," on moving to New York.

Page de droite : « Before the Law Stands a Doorkeeper », une installation en technique mixte réalisée par Patkin peu après son arrivée à New York, occupe tout un mur de sa salle de réunion.

Gegenüberliegende Seite: Im Besprechungsraum steht die wand-große Installation „Before the Law Stands a Doorkeeper", die Patkin in der Zeit schuf, als er nach New York übersiedelte.

Previous pages: Patkin's black-rubber-and-ribbon "Santa Shoshana" presides over the kitchen's stainless-steel island and shop vitrines.
Above: The three-tier dish-rack chandelier in the kitchen holds all manner of usable and decorative glassware.
Right: A glass sculpture that Patkin made with master glassblower Lino Tagliapietra stands near a large Kim MacConnel painting.

Pages précédentes : Une œuvre de Patkin en caoutchouc noir et rubans, « Santa Shoshana », domine l'îlot de cuisine en acier et des vitrines de boutique.
En haut : Le lustre de trois niveaux dans la cuisine arbore toutes sortes de récipients en verre, utilitaires et décoratifs.
À droite : Une sculpture en verre réalisée par Patkin avec le maître souffleur Lino Tagliapietra se dresse près d'une grande toile de Kim MacConnel.

Vorhergehende Seiten: In der Küche hängt „Santa Shoshana", ein Patkin-Werk aus schwarzem Gummi und Bändern.
Oben: Der dreistöckige Leuchter über der Kücheninsel aus Edelstahl wurde aus Geschirrablagen hergestellt. Darauf stapeln sich verschiedenste bunte Gebrauchs- und Dekorationsgläser.
Rechts: Die Glasskulptur schuf Patkin zusammen mit dem italienischen Glasbläser Lino Tagliapietra. Sie steht neben einem riesigen Bild von Kim MacConnel.

New New York Interiors   Izhar Patkin

Le décorateur intérieur Lorenzo Salazar a abandonné Manhattan à contrecoeur pour un appartement de location plus vaste à Brooklyn. Situé dans un immeuble des années 1920 semblant sorti d'un tableau d'Edward Hopper, il était « complètement délabré ». Heureusement, le mari de la propriétaire du salon de manucure au rez-de-chaussée, un excellent entrepreneur en bâtiment, a rapidement remis les 95 mètres carrés en état. Les moulures en plâtre et les plafonds en fer ont pu être sauvés ; des tons frais blancs et gris ont été appliqués dans toutes les pièces à l'exception de la chambre, tapissée d'un papier peint vintage. Un lit sans tête dessiné par Salazar flotte au milieu de celle-ci telle une île douillette. Le salon désormais très glamour inclut un plafonnier géant de George Nelson et un beau miroir espagnol du 17ᵉ siècle. Le décorateur plaisante : « C'était un appartement modeste. C'est ça, la magie de New York : on cligne des yeux et tout a changé ! »

Lorenzo Salazar

Interior Designer Lorenzo Salazar reluctantly abandoned living in Manhattan for a larger Brooklyn rental apartment in a 1920s building straight out of some Edward Hopper painting. "The place was a wreck," the designer says. Fortunately, the owner of the nail salon right downstairs is married to an excellent contractor who deftly repaired the 1,000-square-foot flat. Plaster moldings and tin ceilings were salvaged, and crisp shades of white and gray were applied throughout, except for the vintage wallpaper in the bedroom. Salazar sleeps without a headboard since the bed he designed floats like a plush island in the center of the room. The now-glamorous living room includes an extravagantly scaled George Nelson pendant light and a fine 17th-century Spanish mirror. "This was once a modest apartment. Like all of New York, you blink and it changes," the designer jokes.

Interior-Designer Lorenzo Salazar zog nur ungerne von Manhattan in diese größere Mietwohnung in Brooklyn. Sie liegt in einem Haus aus den 1920ern, das aus einem Edward-Hopper-Bild stammen könnte, und sie war „eine Bruchbude". Ein Glück für Salazar war, dass die Besitzerin des Nagelstudios unten im Haus mit einem ausgezeichneten Bauleiter verheiratet ist. Dieser nahm die Reparaturarbeiten der 95 Quadratmeter großen Wohnung gleich in Angriff: Die originalen Zierleisten aus Gips und die Blechdecken wurden gerettet, die Wände wurden mit verschiedenen klaren Weiß- und Grautönen gestrichen. Einzig im Schlafzimmer hängen noch die alten Tapeten. Dort schwebt das Bett, ein Entwurf Salazars, wie eine friedliche Insel im Raum. Im nun glamourösen Wohnzimmer macht sich die Hängelampe von George Nelson genauso gut wie der spanische Spiegel aus dem 17. Jahrhundert. Der Designer scherzt: „Das war mal eine sehr bescheidene Wohnung, aber wie bei allem in New York, schnipst man mit den Fingern, und es verwandelt sich."

Previous pages: The apartment occupies the entire parlour floor of a building in Williamsburg, Brooklyn.
Above: Salazar added architectural details between the dining and living rooms.
Right: The living room's 20th-century Flemish giltwood convex mirror looms over Salazar's dog Sophee. A Moroccan lantern hangs in the wallpapered bedroom beside a stripped 18th-century French chair.

Pages précédentes : L'appartement occupe tout le premier étage d'un immeuble de Williamsburg, à Brooklyn.
En haut : Salazar a ajouté des détails architecturaux entre le salon et la salle à manger.
À droite : Sophee, la chienne de Salazar, pose sous un miroir convexe flamand en bois doré du 20ᵉ siècle. Dans la chambre tapissée de papier peint, une lanterne marocaine est suspendue près de la carcasse d'une chaise française du 18ᵉ siècle.

Vorhergehende Seiten: Salazars Wohnung in Williamsburg, Brooklyn, umfasst das gesamte erste Obergeschoss.
Oben: Im Durchgang zwischen Ess- und Wohnzimmer brachte Salazar ein paar architektonische Elemente an.
Rechts: Salazars Hund Sophee thront im Wohnzimmer unter einem konvexen Spiegel im vergoldeten flämischen Holzrahmen aus dem 20. Jahrhundert. Im Schlafzimmer: vor der alten Tapete eine marokkanische Laterne und ein abgelaugter französischer Stuhl aus dem 18. Jahrhundert.

Right: *A 19th-century bronze-and-porcelain Chinese export candelabra sits on the mantle. A Karl Springer coffee table holds a Buddha's head and a mercury-glass vessel Salazar turned into a lamp.*
Below: *The living room windows are hung with antique Turkish tapestries over vintage matchstick bamboo scrim.*

À droite : *Sur le manteau de cheminée, un chandelier chinois du 19ᵉ siècle en bronze et porcelaine. Sur une table basse de Karl Springer, une tête de bouddha et un vase en verre argenté que Salazar a monté en lampe.*
En bas : *Les fenêtres du salon sont drapées de tapisseries turques anciennes par-dessus des stores vintage en fibres de bambou.*

Rechts: *Auf dem Kaminsims steht ein chinesischer Kandelaber aus Bronze und Porzellan aus dem 19. Jahrhundert. Auf dem Couchtisch von Karl Springer steht ein Buddha-Kopf. Ein Quecksilberglasgefäß wurde von Salazar in eine Lampe verwandelt.*
Unten: *Antike türkische Wandteppiche als Rollos über altem Bambusfaserstoff an den Wohnzimmerfenstern.*

Facing page: Antique mirrors complement the bathroom's original mirrored medicine cabinet and sconce.
Above: The bedroom's color palette came from a 1961 still life painting Salazar inherited from his grandmother.
Right: The utilitarian kitchen occupies the entry vestibule. The clay sunburst above the stove is from Salazar's native New Mexico.

Page de gauche : Dans la salle de bain, des miroirs anciens sont venus compléter l'ancienne armoire à pharmacie et l'applique qui se trouvaient déjà dans l'appartement.
En haut : Les couleurs de la chambre ont été choisies à partir d'une nature morte de 1961 que Salazar a héritée de sa grand-mère.
À droite : La cuisine, fonctionnelle, occupe l'ancien vestibule. Le soleil en terre cuite au-dessus de la cuisinière vient du Nouveau-Mexique, d'où est originaire Salazar.

Gegenüberliegende Seite: Im Badezimmer hängen diverse antike Spiegel rund um einen alten Medizinschrank und eine Wandlampe.
Oben: Ein Stillleben von 1961, das Salazar von seiner Großmutter erbte, inspirierte ihn für die Farbwahl im Schlafzimmer.
Rechts: Die praktische Küche nimmt den Platz des Vestibüls im Eingang ein. Die Sonne aus Ton über dem Herd hat Salazar aus seiner Heimat New Mexico mitgebracht.

Le nouvel appartement du promoteur immobilier Herbert Sambol, au 12e étage d'une tour en verre et acier de Richard Meier sur West Side Highway, jouit de vues panoramiques sur l'Hudson et le New Jersey. Pour transformer la carcasse vide en élégante garçonnière d'une chambre, il a fait appel au cabinet qui avait déjà conçu sa précédente résidence, Shelton, Mindel & Associates. Afin d'assurer un peu d'intimité dans l'espace entièrement ceint de baies vitrées du sol au plafond, Mindel a créé un bloc central recouvert d'un plaquage en orme pour cacher, entre autres, la salle de bain. Il a également fait entrer les éléments naturels à l'intérieur, avec un sol frais en terrazzo du même bleu vert que le fleuve glacé en contrebas. Sambol adore contempler les tempêtes cingler ses vitres. « Ici, tout là-haut, on est en dehors de soi-même, enveloppé dans la sérénité. »

Herbert Sambol

Real estate developer Herbert Sambol's new twelfth-floor apartment in a glass-and-steel Richard Meier tower on the West Side Highway has panoramic views of the Hudson River and New Jersey. But the space was delivered completely raw, so Sambol commissioned architects Shelton, Mindel & Associates, who had designed his previous apartment, to turn the void into an elegantly spare one-bedroom bachelor pad. Given Meier's floor-to-ceiling glass walls, the designers had to provide some privacy, so they hid the bathroom and other secluded spaces within a freestanding elm-paneled core. Nature played its part in the decoration, with the architects matching the cool blue-green of the terrazzo floor to the ice-filled winter river outside. And Sambol relishes watching storms thrash against those windows: "Up here, you're outside yourself," he says. "The serenity envelops you."

Der Bauunternehmer Herbert Sambol lebt in der zwölften Etage des aus Glas und Stahl errichteten Apartmenthauses von Richard Meier am West Side Highway – mit Panoramablick auf den Hudson River und New Jersey. Sambol kaufte das Apartment im Rohbau und beauftragte das Architekturbüro Shelton, Mindel & Associates, das bereits seine vorherige Wohnung entworfen hatte, daraus eine elegante, geräumige Junggesellenbleibe zu schaffen. Die Apartments in Meiers Bau haben rundum Fensterwände, und so mussten sich die Designer etwas einfallen lassen, um Privatsphäre zu schaffen. Ihre Lösung: Badezimmer und die anderen abgeschlossenen Räume befinden sich in einem mit Ulmenholz vertäfelten Kubus. Für den kühl-graublauen Terrazzoboden ließen sich die Architekten von der Farbe des eisigen, winterlichen Hudson River inspirieren. Sambol liebt es, den an die Fenster peitschenden Stürmen zuzuschauen: „Hier oben fühlt man sich von einer wunderbaren Ruhe umfangen."

Previous pages: A Charlotte Perriand "Tokyo" bench and a "F-1-W" floor lamp by Gilbert Watrous are silhouetted by the view of the Hudson River. The wicker chairs are by Poul Kjærholm.
Above: Since internal partitions do not extend to the exterior walls, no physical barrier divides the bedroom from living spaces.
Right: The Corian bathroom has a quartzite floor.
Facing page: In the bedroom, a Frits Henningsen chair sits against cloud-colored wool voile curtains.

Pages précédentes : Un banc « Tokyo » de Charlotte Perriand et un lampadaire « F-1-W », de Gilbert Watrous, se détachent devant la vue sur le Hudson. La paire de fauteuils en osier de Poul Kjærholm.
En haut : Aucune cloison interne ne s'étendant jusqu'aux murs extérieurs, la chambre est ouverte sur le séjour.
À droite : Dans la salle de bain, les meubles sont en Corian et le sol en quartzite.
Page de droite : Dans la chambre, une bergère « Chair » de Fritz Henningsen se trouve devant des voilages en laine couleur de nuage.

Vorhergehende Seiten: Die „Tokyo"-Bank von Charlotte Perriand und die „F-1-W"-Stehlampe von Gilbert Watrous ergeben zusammen mit der Aussicht auf den Hudson River eine gelungene Bildkomposition. Das Sesselpaar aus Korbgeflecht ist von Poul Kjærholm.
Oben: Die Trennwände sind nicht ganz durchgezogen, so sind Schlafzimmer und Wohnbereich nicht völlig voneinander abgetrennt.
Rechts: Badezimmer aus Corian und mit Quarzitböden.
Gegenüberliegende Seite: Im Schlafzimmer steht ein Sessel von Frits Henningsen vor wolkenfarbenen Voiler-Vorhängen aus Wolle.

Le triplex de l'artiste Andres Serrano à Greenwich Village est un refuge sombre et serein. Un lustre néogothique du 19ᵉ siècle est suspendu au haut plafond du séjour, où la plupart des lourds meubles en bois datent des 16ᵉ et 17ᵉ siècles. Même l'art contemporain, deux photographies signées du maître des lieux, présentent des sujets en costume de la Renaissance. Sa collection inclut de nombreuses statues d'église, dont un saint Jean du 16ᵉ siècle, ancienne pièce de la Norton Simon collection, et un grand Christ allemand en bois du 16ᵉ siècle. Pourtant, Serrano n'a pas cherché à créer un sanctuaire. « Je collectionne l'art et le mobilier du 16ᵉ et 17ᵉ siècles parce que j'aime leur aspect. Si la plupart ont été créés à des fins religieuses, ce n'est pas ce qui m'intéresse ». Néanmoins, il règne dans son appartement monastique une atmosphère paisible de cathédrale.

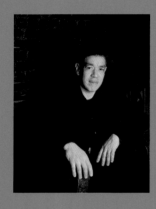

Andres Serrano

Artist Andres Serrano's Greenwich Village triplex is a darkly serene retreat. A 19th-century Gothic Revival chandelier hangs from the high ceiling in the living room. Most of the heavy wood furniture beneath it dates from the 16th and 17th centuries. Even the contemporary art – two Serrano photographs – is of figures in Renaissance-era costume. There are many pieces of church statuary, including a 16th-century St. John, once in the Norton Simon collection, and a large 16th-century German carving of the crucified Jesus. If the atmosphere is overtly religious, that's not Serrano's intention. "I collect 16th- and 17th-century furniture and art because I like the way it looks," he says. "Most of it was made for religious purposes, but that's not why I buy it." Maybe not, but Serrano's monastic apartment is nevertheless filled with a cathedral-like sense of peace.

Im Triplex-Apartment des Künstlers Andres Serrano im Greenwich Village regiert eine düstere, doch gleichzeitig friedliche Welt. Von der hohen Decke des Wohnzimmers hängt ein neugotischer Leuchter, die meisten der schweren Holzmöbel stammen aus dem 16. oder 17. Jahrhundert, und sogar die zeitgenössischen Kunstfotografien von Serrano stellen Figuren in Renaissance-Kostümen dar. Viele der Objekte wirken klerikal wie etwa die Figur des Heiligen Johannes aus dem 16. Jahrhundert, die früher zur Norton-Simon-Sammlung in Pasadena, Kalifornien, gehörte, und die große geschnitzte, gekreuzigte Jesusfigur aus Deutschland. Eine religiöse Aussage ist das nicht: „Ich sammle Möbel und Objekte aus dem 16. und 17. Jahrhundert, weil sie mir gefallen", sagt Serrano. „Die meisten wurden zwar für religiöse Zwecke hergestellt, doch deswegen kaufe ich sie nicht." Wie auch immer: Serranos klerikales Apartment strahlt die Ruhe einer Kathedrale aus.

Previous pages: *A 17th-century Spanish carving of a knight and various other objects form a tabletop vignette.*
Above: *A 16th-century German carving of an almost life-size, but armless, Jesus hangs on the exposed-brick wall in the living room.*
Right: *Serrano's "The Mime," a photograph from his 1996 series, "A History of Sex," hangs on the staircase's limestone wall.*
Facing page: *In the living room, 16th-century Italian ecclesiastical chairs line the walls. The stuffed Siamese cat is named Sybille.*

Pages précédentes : *Un panneau sculpté espagnol du 17ᵉ siècle représentant un chevalier, et d'autres curiosités.*
En haut : *Un Christ allemand du 16ᵉ siècle, presque grandeur nature mais sans bras, est accroché sur le mur en briques nues du séjour.*
À droite : *« The Mime », une photographie de Serrano, appartenant à sa série de 1996 « A History of Sex », orne le mur de l'escalier.*
Page de droite : *Dans le séjour, des sièges ecclésiastiques italiens du 16e siècle bordent les murs. Le chat siamois empaillé s'appelle Sybille.*

Vorhergehende Seiten: *Relief eines Ritters aus Spanien aus dem 17. Jahrhundert und verschiedene andere Objekte.*
Oben: *An der unverputzten Backsteinwand im Wohnzimmer hängt eine fast lebensgroße, armlose, geschnitzte Jesusfigur aus Deutschland aus dem 16. Jahrhundert.*
Rechts: *Serranos Fotografie „The Mime" aus der „A History of Sex"-Serie von 1996 an der Kalksteinwand hinter der Treppe.*
Gegenüberliegende Seite: *Italienische Stühle aus Kirchen aus dem 16. Jahrhundert an den Wohnzimmerwänden. Die ausgestopfte siamesische Katze heißt Sybille.*

Facing page: The mezzanine is faced with paneling from a 19th-century church in New Jersey. Under the mezzanine, tiger-oak paneling from the renovated Excelsior Hotel in Manhattan lines the dining nook, while the table, chairs, and bench are 17th-century English. Serrano replaced the floors with reclaimed wood.

Page de droite : Le garde-corps de la mezzanine est une boiserie provenant d'une église du 19e siècle dans le New Jersey. Dessous, le coin salle à manger est lambrissé d'une boiserie en chêne tigre récupérée dans l'Excelsior Hotel à Manhattan avant sa rénovation. La table, les chaises et le banc sont anglais et datent du 17e siècle. Serrano a recouvert les sols d'un plancher en bois de récupération.

Gegenüberliegende Seite: Das Zwischengeschoss ist mit Paneelen aus einer Kirche des 19. Jahrhunderts in New Jersey verkleidet. Darunter in der Essecke eine Täfelung aus Tigereiche, die aus dem renovierten Excelsior Hotel in Manhattan stammt. Der Tisch, die Stühle und die Bank sind aus England und stammen aus dem 17. Jahrhundert. Serrano verlegte den Boden mit recyceltem Holz.

Above: "Head," a photograph from "A History of Sex," and one of only two Serrano works in the apartment, sits on a 16th-century Italian coffer-bench.
Right: In the bathroom, a 19th-century genre painting of Jesus hangs near a 19th-century mirror flanked by a pair of 19th-century gilded devils.

En haut : « Head », une autre photographie de la série « A History of Sex », la seule autre œuvre de Serrano se trouvant dans l'appartement, est posée sur un coffre/banc italien du 16e siècle.
À droite : Dans la salle de bain, un tableau de genre représentant Jésus est accroché près d'un miroir flanqué de deux diables dorés. Tous datent du 19e siècle.

Oben: „Head" eine Fotografie aus der Serie „A History of Sex" auf einem italienischen Architekturfragment aus dem 16. Jahrhundert. Sie ist neben einer anderen Arbeit das einzige eigene Werk, das Serrano im Apartment ausgestellt hat.
Rechts: Im Badezimmer: ein Jesus-Gemälde neben einem Spiegel, der von einem Paar vergoldeter Figuren, aus dem 19. Jahrhundert, gerahmt wird.

New New York Interiors   Andres Serrano

Les peintures de Philip Taaffe racontent de belles histoires où s'entre-lacent des motifs historiques et naturels disparates. Il a appliqué le même traitement aux huit pièces qu'il habite depuis 1991 dans le Chelsea Hotel. Le locataire précédent, le compositeur et pilier culturel Virgil Thomson, y avait vécu plus de cinquante ans. Pour retenir son karma, Taaffe a racheté certains de ses meubles lors de la vente de ses biens. Avec l'aide du décorateur Ricky Clifton, il est parti d'une base décorative reposant sur un mobilier américain du 19ᵉ siècle, agrémentée de pièces marocaines, syriennes et indiennes. Les murs peints de couleurs vives (« J'ai dû m'y reprendre à plusieurs fois avant de trouver les tons justes », confie-t-il) sont ornés d'une singulière collection d'art qui remonte jusqu'au 15ᵉ siècle. Pourtant, rien dans cet appartement ne paraît affecté.

Philip Taaffe

In his paintings, Philip Taaffe weaves disparate historical and natural motifs into rich visual narratives. Taaffe does something similar in the eight-room Chelsea Hotel apartment he has lived in since 1991. The previous tenant of 50-plus years had been American composer and cultural kingpin, Virgil Thomson. Alert to that rich karma, Taaffe bought back some of Thomson's furniture at his estate sale. Working with designer Ricky Clifton, Taaffe used 19th-century American furniture as a decorative base, interspersed with pieces from Morocco, Syria, and India. He painted the walls bright colors – "It took several attempts to get them right," he says – and hung them with an idiosyncratic art collection that goes back to the 15th century. But there's nothing precious about the rooms, which, after all, Taaffe shares with his wife, Gretchen Carlson, and their two sons.

Philip Taaffe verquickt in seinen Bildern unterschiedliche Motive aus Geschichte und Natur zu reichhaltigen visuellen Erzählungen. Ähnliches machte er mit dem Acht-Zimmer-Apartment im Chelsea Hotel, in dem er seit 1991 lebt. Vor ihm wohnte hier über fünfzig Jahre lang Virgil Thomson, amerikanischer Komponist und Kultfigur. Taaffe kaufte, angetan von dessen starkem Karma, Möbel aus seinem Nachlass. Für die Grundausstattung wählte er zusammen mit dem Designer Ricky Clifton amerikanische Möbel aus dem 19. Jahrhundert – dazwischen platzierte er Objekte aus Marokko, Syrien und Indien. Die Wände hat Taaffe farbig streichen lassen: „Es brauchte aber mehrere Anstriche, bis die Farben stimmten." Dort hängt nun seine eigenwillige Kunstsammlung, die frühsten Werke stammen aus dem 15. Jahrhundert. Gekünstelt wirken die Räume aber nicht – schließlich leben hier auch noch Taaffes Frau, Gretchen Carlson, und ihre beiden Söhne.

Previous pages: The living room's dazzling Persian-blue walls set off a variety of artworks, including Taaffe's 1990 "Desert Flowers."
Right: Taaffe's wife, Gretchen Carlson, and son, William, are framed by an early 15th-century Cenni Francesco di Ser Cenni "St. Catherine" on the right and a 16th-century Dutch Flemish painting in the style of Lucas Cranach on the left.
Below: The Renzo Mongiardino coffee table, sitting on a fine 19th-century Persian rug, is the only 20th-century piece in the living room; the built-in cabinets beyond are original to the hotel.

Pages précédentes : Parmi les œuvres accrochées sur les murs du salon peint en « bleu de Perse », « Desert Flowers » (1990) de Taaffe.
À droite : Gretchen Carlson, l'épouse de Taaffe, et leur fils William se tiennent entre une « Sainte Catherine » de Cenni di Francesco di Ser Cenni (début 15ᵉ siècle), à droite, et un tableau flamand du 16ᵉ siècle dans le style de Lucas Cranach, à gauche.
En bas : La table basse de Renzo Mongiardino, posée sur un tapis persan du 19ᵉ siècle, est le seul meuble du 20ᵉ siècle de la pièce. La bibliothèque encastrée dans le fond appartient à l'hôtel.

Vorhergehende Seiten: Das betörende Persischblau an den Wohnzimmerwänden dient als Hintergrund für eine Reihe von Kunstwerken, zu denen Taaffes „Desert Flowers" von 1990 gehören.
Rechts: Taaffes Frau Gretchen Carlson und Sohn William gerahmt von „heiligen Katharina" von Cenni di Francesco di Ser Cenni aus dem frühen 15. Jahrhundert (rechts) und einem flämischen Gemälde aus dem 16. Jahrhundert im Lucas-Cranach-Stil (links).
Unten: Einziges Objekt aus dem 20. Jahrhundert ist der Couchtisch von Renzo Mongiardino auf einem Perserteppich aus dem 19. Jahrhundert. Die eingebauten Bücherschränke im Hintergrund sind originale Möbelstücke des Hotels.

Above: Paintings by the 17th-century artist Monsù Desiderio hang
above 19th-century cabinets in the library.
Right: The apartment is an enfilade of well-proportioned rooms.
Following pages: The yellow of the dining room's walls is echoed in
the Paul Feeley painting. Clockwise from top left: Moroccan table in
the dining room; a Regency chair once owned by Jacqueline Onassis;
the American Rococo bed belonged to Virgil Thomson; Christopher
Dresser "Persian Garden" china. The beaded curtain was a gift from
Taaffe's Neapolitan gallerist, Lucio Amelio.

En haut : Dans le bureau, des tableaux du 17e siècle de Monsù Desiderio
sont accrochés au-dessus d'une bibliothèque américaine du 19e siècle.
À droite : Une enfilade de pièces aux belles proportions.
Pages suivantes : Le jaune des murs de la salle à manger renvoie au
tableau de Paul Feeley. De gauche à droite dans le sens des aiguilles
d'une montre : dans la salle à manger, une table marocaine ; un fauteuil Regency ayant appartenu autrefois à Jacqueline Onassis ; le lit
rococo américain appartenait à Virgil Thomson ; la vaisselle en porcelaine de Christopher Dresser, « Persian Garden ». Le rideau de perles
fut offert à Taaffe par son galeriste napolitain, Lucio Amelio.

Oben: In der Bibliothek hängen zwei Gemälde von Monsù Desiderio
aus dem 17. Jahrhundert über den Bücherschränken.
Rechts: Eine Flucht von gut proportionierten Räumen.
Folgende Seiten: Das Bild von Paul Feeley nimmt das Goldgelb der
Esszimmerwände auf. Von links im Uhrzeigersinn: ein marokkanischer
Tisch im Esszimmer; ein Regency-Stuhl, der früher Jacqueline Onassis
gehörte; das amerikanische Rokoko-Bett aus Virgil Thomsons Nachlass;
Gebäck auf dem Porzellangeschirr „Persian Garden" von Christopher
Dresser; der Perlenvorhang aus einem algerischen Restaurant ist ein
Geschenk von Philip Taaffes Galeristen in Neapel, Lucio Amelio.

London Terrace, un complexe d'appartements des années 1930 à Chelsea, a eu bien des occupants célèbres. Quand le musicien Rufus Wainwright y a emménagé avec son compagnon, le directeur artistique Jörn Weisbrodt, le locataire qui les avait précédés était le styliste John Bartlett. Weisbrodt, qui a quitté Berlin pour rejoindre son ami, a donc fait expédier ses meubles, qui incluent des chaises de la cafétéria du Berliner Ensemble et une table de Gio Ponti. « Rufus vivait dans un studio, alors que mon ancien appartement faisait 120 mètres carrés ». La famille de Wainwright a également contribué à l'ameublement, sa mère lui ayant donné deux tabourets. Il aimait tellement le lustre qu'il avait offert à sa sœur pour son mariage qu'il s'en est trouvé une réplique plus petite pour la cuisine.

Rufus Wainwright & Jörn Weisbrodt

London Terrace, a 1930s apartment complex in Chelsea, often has well-known residents. When musician Rufus Wainwright and his German boyfriend, arts manager Jörn Weisbrodt, moved into a one-bedroom rental there recently, the previous tenant had been fashion designer John Bartlett. "I shipped my stuff from Berlin," says Weisbrodt, who came to New York to join Wainwright. "Rufus lived in a studio here, while my flat was about 1,300 square feet." So Weisbrodt supplied most of the furniture in the couple's new home. His pieces include chairs from the Berliner Ensemble cafeteria, and a table by Gio Ponti. Wainwright's family contributed items, like two footstools, a gift from his mother. And he so liked the chandelier he gave his sister, Martha, for her wedding, that he got one for the kitchen.

Im Apartmenthaus London Terrace aus den 1930ern in Chelsea lebten bereits viele berühmte Menschen. In der Mietwohnung hatte, bevor der Musiker Rufus Wainwright und der Kunstmanager Jörn Weisbrodt einzogen, der Modedesigner John Bartlett gewohnt. „Meine Sachen ließ ich aus Berlin kommen", sagt Weisbrodt, der nach New York zog, um mit Wainwright zusammenzuleben. Während Weisbrodt in Berlin auf 120 Quadratmetern lebte, bewohnte Wainwright in New York ein kleines Studio. So brachte Weisbrodt das meiste Mobiliar in das neue Zuhause ein. Darunter Stühle der Cafeteria des Berliner Ensembles und ein Tisch von Gio Ponti. Wainwright ergänzte den Hausrat mit zwei Polsterschemeln, ein Geschenk seiner Mutter, und dem Leuchter in der Küche. Das größere Modell schenkte er zuvor seiner Schwester Martha zur Hochzeit.

Facing page: In the bedroom, an autographed vinyl recording of Judy Garland's famous 1961 Carnegie Hall concert, which Wainwright recreated in 2006, sits on an Osvaldo Borsani "P40" armchair.
Left: Photomontages by the Russian artist Roman Ermakov sit on top of the piano, which is in the bedroom.
Below: On the bathroom wall, a poster from each of the four cities – New York, Los Angeles, London, and Paris – in which Wainwright, following Garland, recreated her legendary series of 1961 concerts.

Page de gauche : Sur un fauteuil « P40 » d'Osvaldo Borsani, la pochette dédicacée d'un enregistrement vinyle du célèbre concert de Judy Garland à Carnegie Hall en 1961, dont Wainwright a reprit l'intégralité en 2006.
À gauche : Sur le piano qui se trouve dans la chambre, des photomontages de l'artiste russe Roman Ermakov.
En bas : Sur le mur de la salle de bain, les affiches des quatre villes – New York, Los Angeles, Londres et Paris – où Wainwright, sur les traces de Garland, a recréé sa légendaire série de concerts de 1961.

Gegenüberliegende Seite: Im Schlafzimmer steht auf dem Sessel „P40" von Osvaldo Borsani ein von Judy Garland signiertes Schallplattencover von ihrem legendären Konzert 1961 in der Carnegie Hall.
Links: Fotomontagen des russischen Künstlers Roman Ermakov auf dem Piano im Schlafzimmer.
Unten: Poster von vier Städten – New York, Los Angeles, London und Paris – im Badezimmer. Auf den Spuren Judy Garlands arbeitete Wainwright in diesen Städten an einer Neuversion ihrer legendären Konzertreihe von 1961.

Previous pages: A vintage Poul Henningsen light hangs in the entry hall. Marguerite Friedlaender vase sits on the hall table. Chairs designed by Helene Weigel, Bertold Brecht's wife, for the Berliner Ensemble cafeteria, surround the French 1950s dining table; the painting is by Jonathan Meese. The footstools were designed by Lorca Cohen, Leonard Cohen's furniture-dealer daughter.

Pages précédentes : Un plafonnier de Poul Henningsen éclaire le hall d'entrée. Un vase des années 1930 de Marguerite Friedlaender est posé sur une ancienne table de chevet dans l'entrée. Des chaises dessinées par Helene Wiegel, l'épouse de Bertold Brecht, pour la cafétéria du Berliner Ensemble, entourent une table française des années 1950 ; au mur, une peinture de Jonathan Meese. Les deux tabourets ont été dessinés par Lorca Cohen.

Vorhergehende Seiten: Eine Poul-Henningsen-Hängelampe im Entree. Auf einem ehemaligen Nachttisch im Flur eine Vase von Marguerite Friedlaender. Die Stühle aus Metall und Leder rund um den französischen Esstisch aus den 1950ern hat Helene Weigel, die Ehefrau von Bertold Brecht, für die Cafeteria des Berliner Ensembles entworfen. An der Wand hängt ein Gemälde von Jonathan Meese. Die Polsterschemel sind ein Entwurf von Leonard Cohens Tochter, der Möbelhändlerin Lorca Cohen.

Addresses / Adresses / Adressen

MARIANNE BOESKY & LIAM CULMAN
Marianne Boesky Gallery
(Gallery)
509 West 24th Street
New York, NY 10011
phone: +1 212 680 9889
info@
marianneboeskygallery.com
www.marianneboeskygallery.com

Deborah Berke & Partners Architects
(Architects)
220 Fifth Avenue
New York, NY 10001
phone: +1 212 229 9211
dba@dberke.com
www.dberke.com

MURIEL BRANDOLINI
Muriel Brandolini
(Interior design)
121 West 19th Street, 3D
New York, NY 10010
phone: +1 212 645 5940
muriel@murielbrandolini.com
www.murielbrandolini.com

GERALD DeCOCK
Gerald DeCock
(Hair stylist)
phone: +1 212 337 1254
gerald.decock@gmail.com
www.geralddecock.com

VANESSA DEL RIO
(Adult Website)
www.vanessadelrio.com

Meridee J. S. Hodges
(Interior design and faux finishes)
Mdeesigns Studio
4001 North Ravenswood, #402
Chicago, IL 60613
phone: +1 773 784 2261
info@mdeesigns.com
www.mdeesigns.com

AN EAST VILLAGE TOWN-HOUSE
Paula Hayes
(Landscape designer)
151 First Avenue, #144
New York, NY 10003
phone: +1 212 420 7733
www.paulahayes.com

Selldorf Architects
(Architects)
860 Broadway
New York, NY 10003
phone: +1 212 219 9571
info@selldorf.com
www.selldorf.com

MICHAEL FUCHS
Galerie Haas & Fuchs
(Gallery)
229 Tenth Avenue
New York, NY 10011
phone: +1 212 980 2400

Niebuhrstraße 5
10629 Berlin
Germany
phone: +49 30 8892 9190
contact@haasundfuchs.de
www.haasundfuchs.de

CINDY GALLOP
The Apartment Creative Agency
(Interior designers)
101 Crosby Street
New York, NY 10012
phone: +1 212 219 6331
anne@theapt.com
www.theapt.com

A GARMENT DISTRICT LOFT
Resolution: 4 Architecture
(Architects)
150 West 28th Street, Suite 1902
New York, NY 10001
phone: +1 212 675 9266
info@re4a.com
www.re4a.com

JOEL GREY
(Actor and photographer)
www.joelgreyphotographer.com

FRANÇOIS HALARD
Bastien Halard
(Architect)
info@halard&hallard.com

CONSTANCE HANSEN & RUSSELL PEACOCK
LOT-EK
(Architects)
55 Little West 12th Street
New York, NY 10014
phone: +1 212 255 9326
info@lot-ek.com
www.lot-ek.com

JAN HASHEY & YASUO MINAGAWA
Deborah Berke & Partners Architects
(Architects)
220 Fifth Avenue
New York, NY 10001
phone: +1 212 229 9211
dba@dberke.com
www.dberke.com

Minagawa Art Lines
(Picture framers)
210 Eleventh Avenue, Room 402
New York, NY 10001
phone: +1 212 242 8088

Ineke Hans
(Designer)
Kijkstraat 105
6828 JS Arnheim
The Netherlands
phone: +31 26 389 3892
www.inekehans.com

TYLER HAYS
BDDW
(Furniture gallery)
5 Crosby Street
New York, NY 10013
phone: +1 212 625 1230
info@bddw.com
www.bddw.com

VLADIMIR KAGAN & ERICA WILSON
Vladimir Kagan Design Group
phone: +1 212 289 0031
info@vladimirkagan.com
www.vladimirkagan.com

Erica Wilson
(Needlework)
717 Madison Avenue
63th Street
New York, NY 10021
phone: +1 212 832 7290
www.ericawilson.com

ALEXANDRA & PAUL KASMIN
Paul Kasmin Gallery
(Gallery)
293 Tenth Avenue
New York, NY 10001
511 27th Street
New York, NY 10001
phone: +1 212 563 4474
inquiry@paulkasmingallery.com
www.paulkasmingallery.com

ALEX KATZ
Alex Katz
(Artist)
www.alexkatz.com

TERENCE KOH
Asia Song Society
(Gallery)
www.asiasongsociety.com

CARY LEIBOWITZ
Venturi, Scott Brown & Associates
(Architects)
4236 Main Street
Philadelphia, PA 19127
phone: +1 215 487 0400
info@vsba.com
www.vsba.com

JONATHAN LEITERSDORF
(Architect)
L Capital Partners
10 East 53rd Street, 37th Floor
New York, NY 10022
phone: +1 212 675 7755

9 Ahad Ha'am Street
Shalom Tower
Tel-Aviv 65251
Israel
phone: +972 3 510 8581

SABINE & MICHAEL MAHARAM
Maharam
(Textile showroom)
251 Park Avenue South
New York, NY 10010
phone: +1 212 614 2900
www.maharam.com

Fernlund + Logan Architects
(Architects)
414 Broadway, #7
New York, NY 10013
phone: +1 212 925 9628
www.fernlundlogan.com

LEE MINDEL
Shelton, Mindel & Associates
(Architects)
56 West 22nd Street,
12th Floor
New York, NY 10010
phone: +1 212 206 6406
studio@sheltonmindel.com
www.sheltonmindel.com

Reed A. Morrison Architect
(Architect)
113 Pond Street
Osterville, MA 02655
phone: +1 508 428 8379
ramrama@comcast.net

JULIANNE MOORE & BART FREUNDLICH
MADE
(Architects)
141 Beard Street, Building 12B
New York, NY 11231
phone: +1 718 834 0171
info@made-nyc.com
www.made-nyc.com

JOSH MORTON & SUSAN WEINTHALER
LOT-EK
(Architects)
55 Little West 12th Street
New York, NY 10014
phone: +1 212 255 9326
info@lot-ek.com
www.lot-ek.com

IZHAR PATKIN
Izhar Patkin
(Artist)
www.izharpatkin.com

LORENZO SALAZAR
Studio Salazar
(Interior designer)
288 Graham Avenue, Suite 1
New York, NY 11211
phone: +1 646 216 8107
info@studiosalazar.com

HERBERT SAMBOL
Shelton, Mindel & Associates
(Architects)
56 West 22nd Street,
12th Floor
New York, NY 10010
phone: +1 212 206 6406
studio@sheltonmindel.com
www.sheltonmindel.com

PHILIP TAAFFE
Philip Taaffe
(Artist)
www.philiptaaffe.info

RUFUS WAINWRIGHT & JÖRN WEISBRODT
Lorca/Boo Radley's Antiques
(Lorca Cohen's furniture gallery)
6825 Melrose Avenue
Los Angeles, CA 90038
phone: +1 323 939 6909
info@circa1930.com
www.circa1930.com